ANCIENT JEWISH MYSTICISM

Revived in the So-Called "Light" of the Masonic Lodge: (An exposition of Ezekiel 8) A CHRISTIAN PERSPECTIVE

Donald Huffman

Ancient Jewish Mysticism

tellwell

Tellwell Talent
www.tellwell.ca

ISBN
978-0-2288-9115-4 (Hardcover)
978-0-2288-9114-7 (Paperback)
978-0-2288-9116-1 (eBook)

TABLE OF CONTENTS

FORWARD

Evans Nicholson
Choosing Truth Ministries, 2001.
www.ctmin.org
Canada

With appreciation for this publication by Donald Huffman, I have some comments I've found of value in outreach. The issue is not with Freemasons and their affiliates but with a secret Luciferian system designed to place good people into profound levels of bondage. For Donald Huffman and all of us exposing these sources of spiritual bondage (Ephesians 5:11-13), it involves setting captives free in Jesus. We have numerous examples like Charles Finney and D. L. Moody who moved forward in Jesus only after renouncing their Masonic membership. I can recommend Donald Huffman's publication as a valuable asset in exposing a deadly deception involving Christians and even some pastors in almost every denomination.

When Christians and pastors enter into Freemasonry it's an issue of this compromise challenging their effectiveness for the Gospel. As members we could no longer offer prayer in the name of Jesus as it might offend the other faiths in the Lodge. Rather than proclaiming Jesus as the true Light, Masonic authority teaches that He is a great reformer equal to Buddha and Confucius. In each progressive level, Masons are told to seek 'more of this new light'.

Under these teachings Christians stagnate in their faith while their fellow Masonic brethren may never hear the Gospel from them. In all of the oaths and rituals undertaken by Masons the Lodge intentionally becomes a barrier to Jesus. It becomes a major salvational issue when Christians and pastors are distracted away from Jesus in their own bondage rather than witnessing Jesus to their Masonic brethren.

I was brought up in a Christian home by my grandparents. My grandfather was a Mason and my grandmother was a Worthy Grand Matron in the Eastern Star. Christian Masons from the Church would often come by. I always thought of Freemasonry as a Christian organization, or at least compatible with Christianity. I had never heard anything from the Church to believe otherwise. Later, I would also become a member. *How is it possible that so many Christian members defend it while other Christians are exposing it?* In providing answers we should, again, keep in mind that most members are good people like some of our own parents and grandparents involved in the Lodge. As former Masonic members most of us didn't know we were in bondage until being set free from bondage.

The Masonic organization is a global secret society composed of an inner and outer structure. The inner leadership dictates what information will be taught to the vast majority in the outer structure. Within North American Freemasonry there are thirty-three degrees or levels of advancement. The Blue Lodge is the first three degrees to become a Master Mason. More than seventy-five percent of all Masons will never proceed beyond these first three Blue Lodge degrees. This has been intentionally designed to prevent these Masons from ever learning the inner secrets and Luciferian doctrines of Freemasonry. Universal Grand Pontiff of Scottish Rite Masonry, 33 degree Albert Pike wrote the following in his book, *Morals and Dogma* (1871):

> The Blue Degrees are but the outer court or portico of the Temple. Part of the symbols are displayed there to the Initiate, but he is intentionally mislead by false interpretations. It is not intended that he shall understand them; but it is intended that he shall imagine he understands them. Their true explication is reserved for the Adepts, the Princes of Masonry. (819)

On this same page he further extols the virtues of the High Degrees while expanding upon this deception "… for the mass of those called Masons, … in the Blue Degrees; … will labor in vain …"

Imagine being a member of an organization that systematically lies to you, except you don't know this. Masons become the victims of a carefully designed, deadly deception. Members are distracted from questioning the secrets of the Upper Degrees by the so-called 'good deeds of the Lodge'. We did charity work, were taught moral lessons to be a 'good Mason'. We went to meetings with doctors, politicians and members of our respective Churches. I once defended Freemasonry to other members of my Church based upon these things. They were telling me it wasn't a godly organization. Later I would learn about the growing numbers of members in Canada, America and around the world leaving Freemasonry due to publications like this one by Donald Huffman.

Freemasonry exists because of the oaths and rituals taken the first night in the Lodge. Upon arriving we were told nothing of what would be happening. That first night I entered into an oath bound covenant with the god of Masonry called the Great Architect Of The Universe, GROTU. As a Christian I stood blindfolded before the Worshipful Master of the Lodge with a noose around my neck, half naked, filled with fear and confusion. I had been led by my Conductor to the inner door of the Lodge. The

Worshipful Master called out: "Who goes there?" My Conductor replied: "Evans Nicholson who has long been in darkness now seeks the light of our ancient fraternal order." With a nudge, I agreed this to be true. With these words of agreement to proceed I had renounced Jesus as the Light of my life and the Light of this world. I agreed that I had long been in darkness and was now seeking the light offered in Freemasonry. Remaining blindfolded I was led into the inner Lodge to engage in Masonic rituals. I would repeat the words given to me in an oath of obedience to Freemasonry and the GROTU. Later I would learn that this GROTU is called Lucifer in the Upper Degrees.

Manly Hall, 33 Degree Scottish Rite, is called Freemasonry's greatest philosopher. He shares the following from his book, *The Lost Keys of Freemasonry* (1923):

> When the Mason learns that the key to the warrior on the block is the proper application of the dynamo of living power, he has learned the mystery of his Craft. The seething energies of Lucifer are in his hands and before he may step onward and upward, he must prove his ability to properly apply energy. (48)

The Luciferian Doctrine is that Lucifer never fell and remains in heaven fighting on mankind's behalf. That he is the 'Light-bearer' and the 'Morning Star.' This is only one of the inner doctrines that Masons unknowingly bind themselves to. *This is why Freemasonry is called a deadly deception.*

If only part of these things were true, I had given Satan, legal authority, by way of my words in an agreement with him to have access to my life and my mind. For believers who do these things, Scripture tells us that we end up 'serving two masters', double-minded and unstable in all our ways. My ability to discern between truth and deception had been compromised that first night by entering into major spiritual bondage. This is why, it is often difficult for Christians and pastors to comprehend the deadly deception they are under. As a result, Christians like myself, may end up defending 'doctrines of demons'.

During a two-year period, prompted by questions in my mind, I had been reading everything I could find about Freemasonry. I was confused by the things I couldn't understand or believe. Finally, I read something by a Christian about his former Lodge experience. In my mind I said, *"I can't be a Mason and serve Jesus. I'll never be a Mason again."* I felt something lift off my mind and in a split second I understood the truth in all those books I had been reading. In the days that followed I found a greater clarity in reading my Bible I had not known before. I now knew the gratitude those former Masons expressed towards Jesus for providing freedom from bondage. This also includes those like Donald Huffman, who although never involved in the secret societies, have been led to expose darkness so that captives might be set free in Jesus. For Christians and those receiving Jesus, it comes down to a choice of what is more important in their lives, 'Jesus or the Lodge'?

Dealing with Freemasonry can lead to confrontation, depending on the situation. There are occasions where Church splits have happened or where pastors have been fired by Masons in positions like the Board of Directors. In other situations, it may involve making sure a Mason is saved before dealing with Masonic issues in his life and the problems this often has within the family. I often think of John Bishop, here in British Columbia. John was a 32 degree Mason attending the weekly Christian Full Gospel Business Men's Fellowship luncheon meetings. His Masonic membership was, of course, an issue. When speaking to John about this, he'd say it was a fraternal organization that did charity work. These are the same things most Christian Masons believe and will say, including myself. However, John had a sincere love for Jesus so they continued to welcome him into their fellowship.

As the years passed by, John turned ninety. With age related difficulties he put out an ad for help in his garden work. Dr. Fast, a friend and retired dentist, responded by spending many hours and days helping John. Within this time together John accepted a Christian publication from a former Mason. Two weeks later, John renounced Freemasonry and burned all of his Masonic regalia. He said: *"I didn't know I was in bondage until I was set free from bondage"*. Two years later he said: *"The past two years of my life have been the best years of my life"*. Not long afterward John went home to be in God's eternal presence. Although this happened many years ago, when John spoke of bondage he didn't know he had been under, I instantly knew the same truth from my own bondage. Over the years, since then, I've noted this is a common recurring theme when Christian Masons are set free from occult bondage.

During a sixteen-year period, I hosted an exhibitor's booth at Missions Fest, Vancouver and during that time, three years at Mission Fest Toronto, up until COVID. The booth display was titled: Freemasonry: A Deadly Deception. About seven years ago in Vancouver, a teenage girl walked up to the display banners and read some of the text on them. She was distressed, almost in tears. She told me her family were Christians involved in the Church. She was asking me what was wrong with Freemasonry. She told me, as Christians, her father was in the Masons and she was a Job's Daughter, an organization for teenage girls under the Women's Order of the Eastern Star. In conversation I confirmed their Christian status but gently showed her some of the issues involving her father's membership. I gave her our handouts to take home. The following year a happy, vibrant teenage girl walked by. I recognized her face though I couldn't remember the context, until she said she was out of Job's Daughters and her father was out of Freemasonry. Seeing people set free is the greatest motivation for Donald Huffman, myself and the numerous Christian authors who are exposing darkness.

Freemasonry: Ezekiel Chapter 8

The purpose of this Book is not a Commentary but an Expose to focus on the numerous similarities between the spirituality in Judah just before their captivity under Babylon and the spirit of Freemasonry!

> And in the sixth year (of the captivity of Jehoiachin), in the sixth month, on the fifth day of the month, as I sat in my house (a captive of the Babylonians) with the elders of Judah sitting before me, the hand of the Lord God fell there upon me. 2. Then I beheld, and lo, a likeness of a Man with the appearance of fire; from His waist downward He was like fire, and from his face upward He had the appearance of brightness like gleaming bronze. (Ezekiel 8:1-2)

This vision Ezekiel received from God was probably after he had lain 390 days on his left side to bear the iniquity of Israel and before he began the 40 days on his right side to bear the iniquity of Judah; for now he was sitting in the house, not lying down. Also, can you imagine God giving Ezekiel a vision of why they are in captivity in Babylon and some of the elders of Judah sitting in the house with him might have been part of the group of elders in the vision?

1

RIGHTEOUSNESS AND JUSTICE

Appearance of a man, fire from his waist down and gleaming bronze from his waist up.

FIRE:

> Wherefore we receiving a kingdom which cannot be moved; let us have grace, whereby we may serve God acceptably with reverence and godly fear. FOR GOD IS A CONSUMING FIRE. (Hebrews 12:28-29)
>
> (Amp. Says – "acceptable worship". Read Rev. 1:14, 15.)

GLEAMING BRONZE:

> RIGHTEOUSNESS AND JUSTICE are the foundation of Your throne;... (Psalm 89:14) |
>
> Therefore thus says the Lord God, Behold, I am laying in Zion for a foundation a Stone, a tested Stone, a precious Cornerstone of sure foundation, he who believes (trusts in, relies on, and adheres

> to that stone) will not be ashamed or give way or hasten away (in sudden panic). I WILL MAKE JUSTICE THE MEASURING LINE AND RIGHTEOUSNESS THE PLUMMET; and hail will sweep the refuge of lies, and WATERS WILL OVERWHELM THE HIDING PLACE. (Isaiah 28:16-17)

The Bronze Altar speaks of JUDGEMENT, JUSTIFICATION, SANCTIFICATION, and IDENTIFICATION AND DAILY CLEANSING! Ahab not only removed the Brazen Altar but replaced it with a heathen altar! (Read 2 Kings 16:10-16) The Brazen Altar is where we start our journey to God, by identification that we have sinned, and by the Sacrificial Lamb we are covered by the "Sinless Blood" He shed:

> The next day John saw Jesus coming to him and said, Look! There is the Lamb of God, Who takes away the sin of the world! (John 1:29)

> (All) are justified and made upright and in right standing with God, freely and gratuitously by His grace (His unmerited mercy and favour), through the redemption which is (provided) in Christ Jesus. Whom God put forward (before the eyes of all) as a mercy seat and propitiation by His blood (the cleansing and life-giving sacrifice of atonement and reconciliation; to be received) through faith… (Romans 3:24-26)

The results of God's judgement on Israel and Judah are evident in their captivity under Babylon!

2

IMAGE OF JEALOUSY

And He put forth the form of a hand and took, me by a lock of my head; and the Spirit lifted me up between the earth and the heavens and brought me in the visions of God to Jerusalem, to the entrance of the door of the inner (court) which faces toward the north, where was the seat of the idol (image) of jealousy, which provokes to jealousy. And behold, there was the glory of the God of Israel (Who had loved and chosen them), like the vision I saw in the plain. Then He (the Spirit) said to me, Son of man, now lift up your eyes toward the north. So I lifted up my eyes toward the north, and behold, on the north of the altar gate was that idol (image) of jealously in the entrance. (Ezekiel 8:3-5)

(References to the images of Baal, that Manasseh, the son of Hezekiah had set up and others are: 2 Kings 16:10–16, 2 Kings 21:4-7, 2 Chron. 33:1-3, and 2 Kings 33:8-11)

Whatever image it was, it was in the highest degree offensive to God, and provoked Him to jealousy and ultimately judgement! And now God appeals to Ezekiel whether this "Image of Jealousy" present, alone was sufficient enough grounds for God to cast off Israel and Judah! I believe the "IMAGE OF JEALOUSY" was both the "IMAGE OF THE PHALLUS" and the "IMAGE OF THE SUN" from the above references! Both are one and the same! One is the "IMAGE OF JEALOUSY IN THE MICROCOSM, and the other, the "IMAGE OF JEALOUSY" in the macrocosm! In Baal worship, the Phallus is worshipped as the MALE GENERATIVE PRINCIPLE whose essence brings for the life in the FEMALE PASSIVE PRINCIPLE (Eteis) in the form of children, and this everlasting life they worship; in a sense, is progressive life through procreation in the microcosm! In the macrocosm, the Sun is worshipped (Baal worship) as the Male Generative Principle whose essence (heat) brings for life in all its various forms through Mother Earth or Mother Nature otherwise called the Female Passive Principle! THIS IS PART OF BAAL WORSHIP AND THE PRINCIPLES (i.e., THE PHALLUS AND THE SUN) ARE THE CHIEF IMAGES THAT ARE WORSHIPPED! God finds these images very offensive and provokes Him to jealousy, judgement and wrath! Why! Because THESE HAVE DIRECTLY TAKEN THE PLACE OF GOD AS CREATOR AND GIVER OF LIFE!!! God is Creator of all life, Sustainer of that which He created and Redeemer of His creation! This is THE FOUNDATION of the GOSPEL:

> (Now) He is the exact likeness of the unseen God (the invisible representation of the invisible); He is the first born of all creation. FOR IT WAS IN HIM THAT ALL THINGS WERE CREATED, IN HEAVEN AND ON EARTH, THINGS SEEN AND THINGS UNSEEN, whether thrones, dominions, rulers, or authorities; ALL

THINGS WERE CREATED AND EXIST THROUGH HIM (by His service, intervention) AND IN AND FOR HIM. And He Himself existed before all things, AND IN HIM ALL THINGS CONSIST (COHERE, ARE HELD TOGETHER). (Col. 1:15-17)

If the foundations are destroyed, what can the (unyieldingly) righteous do, or what he He (THE RIGHTEOUS ONE) wrought or accomplished? (Psalm 11:3)

(Read 2 Kings 21:7)

In the beginning (before all time) was the Word (Christ), and the word was with God, and the word was God Himself. He was present originally with God. 3. ALL THINGS WERE MADE AND CAME INTO EXISTENCE THROUGH HIM; AND WITHOUT HIM WAS NOT EVEN ONE THING MADE THAT HAS COME INTO BEING. 4. IN HIM WAS LIFE, AND LIFE WAS THE LIGHT OF MEN. 5. And the Light shines on in the darkness, for the darkness has never overpowered it (put it out or absorbed it or appropriated it and is unreceptive to it.) (John 1:1-5)

More will be said later about the chief images of Baal Worship, namely the Phallus and the Sun in connection with Freemasonry. For Freemasonry and Baal Worship are identical!

3

EVERY FORM OF CREEPING THINGS

> Furthermore, (The Spirit) said to me, Son of man, do you see what they are doing? The great abominations that the house of Israel is committing here to drive Me far from my sanctuary? But you shall again see greater abominations. And He brought me to the door of the court; and when I looked, behold, there was a hole in the wall. Then He said to me, Son of man, dig now in the wall. And when I had dug in the wall, behold, there was a door. And He said to me, Go in and see the wicked abominations that they do here. So I went in and saw their PICTURES OF EVERY FORM OF CREEPING THINGS AND LOATHSOME BEASTS AND ALL THE IDOLS OF THE HOUSE OF ISRAEL, PAINTED ROUND ABOUT ON THE WALL. (Ezekiel 8:6-10)

The picture on the next page is taken from *A New Encyclopedia of Freemasonry (ars Magna Latomorum) and of Cognate Instituted Mysteries: Their Rites, Literature and History*, by Arthur Edward Waite.

A NEW ENCYCLOPEDIA OF
FREEMASONARY
(ARS MAGNA LATOMORUM0
AND OF COGNATE INSTITUTED
MYSTERIES: THEIR RITES
LITERATURE AND HISTORY by
ARTHUR EDWARD WAITE, P.M., P.Z.
PAST SENIOR GRAND
WARDEN OF IOWA
PAST PROVINCIAL DEPUTY
GRAND DIRECTOR OF
CEREMONNIES (BUCKS.)
PAST GRAND INNER GUARD
(ENGLISH GRAND MARK)
PAST GREAT CAPTAIN
OF THE GUARDS
PAST GRAND HISTORIOGRAPHER
ETC., ETC.
AUTHOR OF “THE SECRET
TRADITION IN FREEMASONRY,” ETC.

Image: Temple of the Mysteries

TEMPLE OF THE MYSTERIES

The Religion of Freemasonry is "pure Theism". In the *Webster's New Collegiate Dictionary*, "Theism" is defined as "belief in the existence of a God or gods; specific: belief in the existence of one God viewed as the creative source of man and the world who transcends yet is imminent in the world." Again, in the *Webster's Dictionary,* "Immanent" here is defined as "remaining or operating within a domain of reality or realm or discourse.

In other words, Freemasonry believes in a god as a creative source, but that god is in the domain of reality or a natural god! Hence, god is in everything right down to the lowest forms of "creeping things and loathsome beasts." (There are some comments by Edmond Ronayne in his excellent expose of Freemasonry entitled *The Master's Carpet* and comments on a number of references from authoritative Masonic books, on pages 73-78.)

> If a soul swear, pronouncing with his lips to do evil or to do good *whatsoever it be that a man shall pronounce with an oath and it be hid from*

> *him* when he knoweth of it then he shall be guilty in one of these, and it shall be when he shall be guilty in one of these things that he shall confess that he had sinned in that thing. (Lev. V., 4, 5)

Freemasonry says to every candidate; "swear although what you called upon to swear to is hidden from you." The Word of God on the other hand says "if you do this you sin against God and you shall be guilty." *The religion of freemasonry is* PURE THEISM, *acknowledging A GOD but denying revelation.* This is very clearly asserted under the work "Religion" in the *Lexicon of Freemasonry*, by A.G. Mackey (1845):

> THE RELIGION THEN OF MASONRY IS PURE THEISM on which its different members engraft their own peculiar opinions, but they are not permitted to introduce them into the lodge or to connect their truth or falsehood with the truth of Masonry. (404)

And when the Jew, the Mahomedan and the Unitarian are initiated, or when they visit a lodge, what does Masonic law require them to "exclude" from the system? Nothing; absolutely nothing. Their religion, if they have any, *is pure theism,* already, and consequently they compromise religiously by being made Masons. But when a Christian minister is made a Mason and lives up to his obligations, what is he called upon to exclude and what does he maintain and support? He must "carefully exclude all sectarian tenets." That is he cannot use the name of Jesus Christ in the lodge room in connection with any Masonic prayer or religious ceremony. He cannot introduce any of, what Masonry calls, his peculiar Christian opinions into the lodge, "nor connect their truth of Masonry," and hence he wilfully compromises his Christian character.

But what is "pure theism?" Polytheism we know is a belief in *many* gods, Atheism is a belief in no God at all, and theism is the belief in a God, and hence Dr Mackey uses the term pure theism in this place, evidently to assert that the religious philosophy of Freemasonry merely recognizes the existence of a something which it calls god, but which is not to be understood as embodying a plurality of persons in that god; or, in other words, it is a denial of the Trinity.

Freemasonry, as we shall find hereafter, is the "secret worship" of paganism revived, and this doctrine of pure theism enunciated here by the Masonic lexicon is simply the same principle which in all pagan countries distinguished their secret from their public worship. This same idea of the Masonic religion is elsewhere referred to by Mackey and others, as "the unity of God," and, together with the doctrine of immortality, is claimed to constitute the sole religious belief of the Masonic philosophy. Referring to these doctrines, and the manner in which they were communicated and preserved in early times, *The Symbolism of Freemasonry*, by Dr. Mackey (1882), states as follows:

> But those among the masses – and there were some – who were made acquainted with the truth, received their knowledge by means of an initiation into certain sacred mysteries in the bosom of which it was concealed from the public gaze. (15)

Hence, then, the pure theism which constitutes the sum and substance of the Masonic philosophy is precisely the same doctrine and mode of faith which is claimed to have existed in the pagan mysteries, after the dispersion of mankind in the plains of Shinar; and to this pagan philosophy of the lodge every candidate, be he minister or layman, "must, with reverence, most humbly bow," according to the tenor of his obligation. In the *Digest of Masonic*

Law by Geo. Wingate Chase (insert publication date here), the Turks, each reject either the New Testament or the Old, or both, and yet we see no good reason why they should not be made Masons. In fact Blue Lodge Masonry has nothing whatever to do with the Bible: "It is not founded upon the Bible. If it was, it would not be Masonry, it would be something else." (insert page number of quote here) During the Tribulation Period, the Antichrist will come on the scene! Masonic Law requires every mason including Christian masons to "CAREFULLY EXCLUDE ALL SECTARIAN TENETS." The Antichrist will do exactly that, by excluding everything that is called God, MAGNIFY HIMSELF ABOVE ALL, BUT WILL HONOUR THE GOD FORTRESSES OR FORIFICATIONS! THIS IS THE GOD OF FREEMASONRY – "THE GREAT ARCHITECT OF THE UNIVERSE"! The Book of Daniel says:

> And the king shall do according to his will; HE SHALL EXALT HIMSELF AND MAGNIFY HIMSELF ABOVE EVERY GOD and shall prosper till the indignation be accomplished, for that which is determined (by God) shall be done.37. He shall not regard the gods of his fathers' or him (to whom) women desire (to give birth- the Messiah), or any other god, for he shall magnify himself above all.38. But in their place he shall honour the god of fortresses; a god whom his fathers knew not shall be honour with gold and silver, with precious stones, and with pleasant and expensive things. (Daniel 11:36-38)

Notice what the Bible says about the Antichrist. It says, he will magnify himself ABOVE ALL, NOT magnify himself AS GOD, but "ABOVE EVERY god' and SPEAK AGAINST THE GOD of gods!

4a

CHRISTIANS IN FREEMASONRY

> And there stood before these (pictures) SEVENTY MEN OF THE ELDERS OF THE HOUSE OF ISRAEL, and in the midst of them stood Jaazaniah the son of Shaphan (the scribe), with every man his censer in his hand, and a thick cloud of incense was going up (in prayer to these their gods). (Ezekiel 8:11)

(Note: The seventy elders in years past (Exodus 24:9; Number 11:16, 17) were to perform as their chief duty to guard against idolatry! What they were worshipping, was a shocking outright perversion of their high calling! One who led them in their depraved devotions was Jaazaniah, one of the sons of Shaphan (the scribe). Shaphan was the man who read the "Book of the Law" personally before King Josiah (2 Kings 22:8-14).)

Unfortunately, THERE ARE MANY CHRISTIANS AND EVEN CHRISTIAN MINISTERS WHO ARE AND WERE ALSO MASONS! I have counselled a good number of them personally! One particular day, for example, I attended the Annual Meeting of the Creation Science Association of Ontario of which I was a director and secretary for a time. While I was in Toronto, attending this meeting at Kennedy Road Tabernacle, I had an appointment arranged so I could talk to the Senior Pastor of Queensway Cathedral (Pastor Rutledge) about the influx of masons in the P.A.O.C. churches. At the end of the C.S.A.O. meeting, I asked a certain person for the easiest direction to Queensway and during our conversation I mentioned my purpose of going there. I.e.to talk about Freemasonry in the churches. The man without hesitation said to me, "Oh, I am a Knights Templar!" From the Masonic book, *Whence Come We? From 1855-1980*, it stated that fifty-four percent OF ALL CORNERSTONES LAID BY MASONIC RITUAL WERE OF CHRISTIAN CHURCHES!

4b

SOME DISTINGUISHED PEOPLE WHO WERE MASONS. ALSO, SOME INFORMATION ON THE GROWTH OF MASONIC LODGES AROUND THE TIME OF CONFEDERATION AND ON

Here are the Early Constitutions and Lodges in Upper Canada from *Constitutions of the Ancient Fraternity of Free and Accepted Masons,* by William Williams, Esq. (1823):

CONSTITUTIONS

OF THE

ANTIENT FRATERNITY

OF

FREE AND ACCEPTED MASONS

PART THE SECOND,

CONTAINING

THE CHARGES, REGULATIONS

&c. &c.

PUBLISHED BY

THE AUTHORITY OF THE UNITED GRAND LODGE,

BY

WILLIAM WILLIAMS, ESQ.

PROVINCIAL GRAND MASTER FOR
THE COUNTY OF DORSET

FIRST CANADIAN EDITION

REPUBLISHED BY ORDER OF THE
PROVINCIAL GRAND LODGE OF

UPPER CANADA

KINGSTON:

PRINTED BY H.C. THOMSON

MDCCCXXIII

THE CONSTITUTION OF GRAND LODGE:

Early Constitutions

The first book of *Constitutions of the Premier Grand Lodge* was prepared by James Anderson, D.D., and issued in 1723. The second edition appeared in 1738, and later revisions followed. The constitution of the Grand Lodge of England (Ancients) bore the curious name of "Ahiman Rezon; or a Help to a Brother". The earliest version, by Laurence Dermott, was published in 1756, and subsequent editions were issued from time to time. Early Provincial Grand Lodges in Canada were governed by one or the other of these books. Copies, which were scarce, had to be imported from England. The first such book published in Upper Canada appeared in 1823, under the auspices of the Second P.G.L. Its title-page ran as follows:

> Constitutions/of/Ancient Fraternity of Free and Accepted Masons, / Part the Second: /Containing/ the Charges, Regulations, /&c, &c.; /Published by/the authority of the United Grand Lodge,/ by/William Williams, Esq.,/Provincial Grand Master for the County of Dorset;/First Canadian Edition;/Republished by Order of the Provincial Grand Lodge of/Upper Canada./Kingston:/ Printed by H.C. Thomson;/MDCCCXXIII.

This was an unaltered reprint of the *Book of Constitutions,* as approved by the United Grand Lodge of England in 1815, and issued in a corrected edition in 1819 (though it was called "Part of the Second," the first Part, which was to have treated of the History of Masonry, was never issued.)

The Constitutions of 1855 and 1856

When the independent Grand Lodge of Canada was instituted in 1855, it needed a constitution. A drafting committee was set up under the chairmanship of V.W. Bro. William Mercer Wilson. The next day on its recommendation, the Constitution of the United Grand Lodge of England was adopted *mutatis mutandis.* As this was clearly provisional, a revising committee was appointed to report at the first Annual Communication in July 1856. The amended Constitution was thoroughly debated, adopted, and ordered to be printed. While many of the articles were taken word for word from the Constitutions of the Second P.G.L. (Premier Grand Lodge), others were altered to meet fresh circumstances. Some of the changes were as follows:

(a) The principal officers of Grand Lodge were to be elected by ballot without nomination, instead of being appointed;
(b) A brother was to be ineligible for election as Grand Master for a third consecutive term (this was rescinded in 1857);
(c) The Deputy Grand Master was to be elected from a part of the Province other than where the Grand Master resided (this refers to Canada East and Canada West);
(d) Not only was each Past Master given one vote at the Annual Communication of Grand Lodge, each lodge was assigned three votes. (176)

History of Grand Lodge, A.F. & A.M. of Canada in the Province of Ontario (Appendix A)

This table shows the growth in membership and finances from 1856 to 1955. The decrease in the number of lodges in 1874 is accounted for by the transfer and cancellation of certain lodges thereafter registered with the Grand Lodge of Quebec. The drop in assets on General Account in 1865 was caused by the withdrawal of $6,000 to establish a Benevolent Fund. In 1889 the amount to the credit of the Benevolent Fund was transferred back to the General Account. In 1902 the amount at the credit of the asylum fund was transferred to the General Account:

Year	No. Of Lodges	Membership
1856	41	1,179
1857	49	1,581
1858	113	3,042
1859	123	3,341
1860	140	3,664
1861	151	3,993
1862	154	4,368

1863	158	4,750
1864	164	5,249
1865	172	5,792
1866	172	6,380
1867	184	7,000
1868	195	8,022
1869	209	8,797
1870	229	9,991
1871	253	1,500
1872	281	12,168
1873	297	13,750
1874	276	14,530
1875	288	15,934
1876	203	16,719
1877	319	17,220
1878	324	17,418
1879	334	17587
1880	340	17,474
1881	346	17,635
1882	347	17,967
1883	349	18,442
1884	350	18,911
1885	356	18,983
1886	357	19,256
1887	357	19,450
1888	355	19,740

Freemasons are heavily involved in politics and boast Royal involvement and people of high government positions that are members of the Craft. The following "Masonic Chronology" is from the *Encyclopaedia of Freemasonry* by Arthur Edward Waite (1791), a high ranking Mason:

> Carolina, one Lodge each; at South Carolina two Lodges, and one at Georgia ...The Ancients warranted a PROVINCIAL GRAND LODGE OF QUEBEC UNDER PRINCE EDWARD, AFTERWARDS DUIKE OF KENT ... THE PROVINCE OF CANADA WAS DIVIDED INTO UPPER AND LOWER CANADA, UNDER PROVINCIAL GRAND MASTERS APPOINTED BY THE ANCIENTS. (78)

Some information on the Grand Lodge of Canada in Ontario is taken from the Masonic book below, *Beyond the Pillars: More Light On Freemasonry*, edited by The Special Committee on Publications (date of publication):

BEYOND THE PILLARS

More Light on Freemasonry

Edited by

THE SPECIAL COMMITTEE
ON PUBLICATIONS

GRAND LODGE A.F. & A.M. OF CANADA
IN THE PROVINCE OF ONTARIO

PUBLISHED BY AUTHORITY OF THE GRAND MASTER

AUDI VIDE TACE
BEYOND THE PILLARS

More Light on Freemasonry
Edited by

THE SPECIAL COMMITTEE ON PUBLICATIONS

Grand Lodge A.F. & A.M. of Canada
In The Province of Ontario
Published by Authority of the Grand Master

The first resolution declared in favour of the principle, and the second in a very few words brought into being that organization which now permeates every corner of our Province, and ranges under its banner no fewer than 115,000 members. It read as follows:

> That we, the representatives of regularly warranted Lodges, have in convention assembled resolved that the Grand Lodge of Ancient, Free and Accepted Masons of Canada be and is hereby formed upon the ancient charges and constitutions of Masonry. (page number required)

To this resolution there was not one dissenting voice. Step by step the work of organization proceeded, and the evening session concluded with the appointment of a committee, headed by William Mercer Wilson, to prepare a constitution for the newly formed Grand Lodge. On the following morning the committee reported and the draft constitution was adopted. Then followed the election of officers, and the meeting showed its gratification in no mistakable manner when it was announced that William Mercer Wilson was elected the first Grand Master of the Grand Lodge of Canada. The business of the convention concluded in harmony by the appointment of a committee to make the necessary arrangements for the installation of the Grand Master-elect.

IN THE PROVINCE OF ONTARIO CHAPTER II: BIRTH OF AN INDEPENDENT GRAND LODGE OF CANADA

An appeal was first made to a Past Grand Master of the Grand Lodge of New York to perform the installation ceremony, but the Grand Master did not think it prudent to advise him to accept the invitation; so the committee proceeded to Detroit where their request was readily granted. The Honourable H.T. Backus, Past Grand Master of the Grand Lodge of Michigan, graciously accepted the invitation. Accordingly, at a special meeting held in the Masonic Hall in Hamilton, on the 2nd of November, 1855, the new Grand Lodge was duly constituted under the name of "The Most Worshipful, The Grand Lodge of Ancient, Free and Accepted Masons of Canada" and William Mercer Wilson, in due and ancient form was installed as the first Grand Master thereof. After tendering to Bro. Backus the thanks of the Grand Lodge for his fraternal kindness in performing the ceremony of consecration and installation in such an impressive manner, the M.W. the Grand Master closed the Grand Lodge in ample form with solemn prayer. The first act of the Grand Master was to forward an address to the Grand Lodge of England in which he reiterated the causes leading up to the formation of the Grand Lodge. He set forth in clear and convincing language the discourteous neglect of the mother Grand Lodge to acknowledge the many appeals that were made to her and concluded as follows:

> Engaged in one common cause – the good of our fellow-men, by promoting the interests of our time-honoured institution, and it being our first wish and highest ambition to establish and perpetuate a sincere and intimate alliance with the Grand Lodge of England, we extend to you, in the name of our divine art, the right hand of brotherhood and confidently claim from you a reciprocation of our fraternal regard.

The following is from the book, *Whence Come We: Freemasonry in Ontario 1764-1980,* edited by Wallace MacLeod, in regards to Royalty, the Prime Ministers of Canada, and some other notable people:

Whence Come We?

Freemasonry in Ontario 1764-1980

Edited by

The Special Committee
on the History;
Wallace McLeod, Chairman

Grand Lodge A.F. & A.M. of Canada
in the Province of Ontario

Published by Authority of the Grand Master

CHAPTER 5

"Monarchs Themselves have been promoters of the Art"

. . . To so high an eminence has its credit been advanced that in every age monarchs themselves have been promoters of the art; have not thought it derogatory from their dignity to exchange the sceptre for the gavel, have patronized our mysteries and have joined our assemblies.

—*Charge to the Newly Initiated Candidate*

WHENCE COME WE?
FREEMASONRY IN ONTARIO 1764-1980
Edited by
The Special Committee on the History;
Wallace McLeod, Chairman
Grand Lodge A.F. & A.M of Canada in the Province of Ontario

> ...To so high an eminence has its credit been advanced that in every age monarchs themselves have been promoters of the art; have not thought it derogatory from their dignity to exchange the sceptre for the gavel, have patronized our mysteries and have joined our assemblies—Charge to the Newly Initiated Candidate.

Before the accession of Queen Victoria

Every Freemason in the Province of Ontario has heard these words many times. He may well have wondered whether there was any truth in the assertions. As a matter of fact they are completely true. This particular claim was first made in the oldest version of the charge, published in 1735 (see below, page 78): "The greatest Monarchs in all Ages, as well as Asia and as of Europe, have been Encouragers of the Royal Art; and many of them have presided as Grand-Masters over the Masons in their respective Territories, not thinking it any lessening to their Imperial Dignities to Level themselves with their Brethren in Masonry, and to act as they did". At the time these words were written they no doubt referred to tales then current about the early history of the Craft. The Old Manuscript Charges mention several patrons of Masonry in addition to S.K.I. and H.K.T.: Nimrod King of Babylon, an unnamed King of Egypt, Charles Martel "King of France", and Athelstan King of England.

To be sure, the alleged connection of these worthies with Freemasonry will hardly bear scrutiny. But happily, since the beginning of modern Masonry in 1717, a total of twenty-three princes of the British royal family have joined the craft, and nine have actually served as Grand Masters. Five of the Kings of Great Britain have been masons.

Note:- I do not wish to name the following leaders in our nation and their years of service to the Masonic Lodge from the book (Whence Come We?), but will only mention numbers. Prominent Prime Ministers -6, Lieutenant Governors -8, Premiers of Ontario -13, Clergymen – dozens!

Appendix

Lodges currently on the Register of the Grand Lodge of Canada in the Province of Ontario which received their original Authorization to meet from an Authority other than the Grand Lodge of Canada.

Column 1: present name, number and location. Column 2: date of warrant, provincial warrant, petition, first meeting, or earliest mention. Column 3: number on the Provincial Register of Jarvis's P.G.L, or of the schismatic P.G.L. of Niagara (1792-1817). Column 4: number on the Provincial Register of McGillivray's P.G.L. (1822-1840). Column 5: number on the Provincial Register of MacNab's P.G.L. (1844-1858). Column 6: number under the Irish Constitution. n.n.: working under the P.G.L., but not numbered. D.: dormant during the period of activity of the P.G.L.

CEREMONY OF LAYING A CORNER-STONE

The corner-stone of the Church of St. Martin in the Fields, London was laid with Masonic ceremonies in 1722. So were those of the Parliament House in Dublin (1729), the Royal Infirmary in

Edinburgh (1738), and the Royal Exchange in Edinburgh (1753). The procedures are outlined in Preston's *Illustrations of Masonry* (1801 ed.) As Masonry spread, the practice of laying corner-stones went with it. The earliest in the Western Hemisphere was that of Fort James, Antigua, in the Leeward Islands, laid on November 15, 1739. BRETHREN OF THE UNITED STATES PROUDLY RECALL THE PART PLAYED BY TH CRAFT IN BUILDING THE WHITE HOUSE (1792) AND THE CAPITAOL (1793). Further north, in Quebec City, the P.G.L. of Lower Canada laid corner stones for the Union Hotel (1805), the new Jail (1809), and St. John's Presbyterian Church (1816). McGillivray's Constitutions of 1823 describe the procedures to be followed at the public ceremony of laying a foundation stone. Many of the instructions are taken verbatim from Preston's Illustrations of Masonry. On May 17, 1824 the P.G.L. of Upper Canada assembled at Kingston, for the foundation of the Midland District Court House and Jail. Over the next thirty-two years, eleven corner-stones were laid with Masonic honours in what is now Ontario. Five were for town halls, etc.

PROVINCIAL GRAND LODGE OF LOWER CANADA (ANCIENTS)

The first meeting of an Ancients Lodge in Quebec was 1785, when part of the Fourth Battalion of the Royal Artillery was stationed there. It had a lodge attached to it, No. 213. (The lodge purchased warrant No. 9 in 1787; it became a civilian lodge in 1829; and is still working as Albion Lodge, No. 2, G.R.Q.) Another detachment of the Royal Artillery station in Quebec received Ancients warrant No. 241 in 1787. (It is still working as St. John Lodge, No. 3, G.R.Q.).

Prince Edward, later Duke of Kent (1767 - 1820), the father of Queen Victoria, came to Canada in 1791. He received a warrant as P.G.M. of Lower Canada from the Grand Lodge of England

(Ancients), dated March 7, 1792. His prestige added to the lustre of the Ancients, and most of the earlier Moderns lodges simply died out. Some thirty lodges were warranted under his P.G.L. Of these four were in the Upper Province: Glengarry, Glengarry Lodge, No. 1 (warranted 1792), Edwardsburgh, Royal Edward Lodge, No. 5 (warranted 1792). Detroit, Zion Lodge, No. 10 (warranted 1794), and Perth, True Britons' Lodge (granted a dispensation 1818).

Note: With this extensive preamble, it is now time to take a closer look at Ontario. I have inserted the following few pages for a number of reasons with relation to the seventy elders God showed Ezekiel in the Temple! From the Masonic book, *Whence Come We: Freemasonry in Ontario 1764-1780*, I'll say again, they stated that 54% of the Ceremonies of Laying a Cornerstone were laid on Church Buildings!!! There are many Masons in the church and many involved in Christian organizations such as the Canadian Bible Society! Honourable Dr. Gordon L. Bennett, for example, is not only a 33rd degree Mason of the Scottish rite (Sovereign Grand Commander). but also, a Member of the Masonic Supreme Council of Canada! Only 2 Masons in all of Canada can hold that position!)

As you will see, the 33 degree Mason by Ritual and Binding Oaths to Death are bound by Masonic Law to be anti-Christian and anti-Supernatural, etc.! While at the same time being one of the highest ranking Masons in the world, he also holds the Honourary position of National President of the Canadian Bible Society! I sent a letter to the General Secretary with a package of information about the 33 degrees. William R. Russell's reply concerning Dr. Bennett was even more astounding!

THE SUPREME COUNCILLOR

Above, is the Emblem of The Supreme Council 33 degrees A. &A. S.R. of Freemasonry of Canada. Below, is an explanation of the words "Deus Meumque Jus", by the highest of Masonic authority and who rewrote the degrees of the Scottish rite which are still in use today. The following is a translated extract from a document addressed to all the Supreme Councils of the World by Albert Pike who was Sovereign Pontiff of Universal Freemasonry. Delivered in Paris, October, 1885, Quoted by Domenico Marotta, a 33 degree Mason, in "Le Culte de la Nature dans la Franc-maconnerie Universelle" – pg. 51: -

D. M. J.

The order demands the immediate enforcement of the D. M. J. Nevertheless (Deus Meumque Jus)

"At different epochs of the life of the nations which have the good fortune of possessing an active Supreme Council, and from 1820 onwards, certain similar communications have been made to certain chosen members of the Grand Consistories and Supreme Councils respectively. It is necessary to give the secret of this order.

"Exoterically D...M...J... are the initials of the words, Destruction, Materialism, Imposition, which 'Impose Destruction of everything which resists Materialism.'

"The three points... mean that the Masonic work of Destruction, Materialism and Imposition is triple:

> Destruction – of Supernaturalism, of Authority, of Anti-Masonic activity.
>
> Materialism – of Conscience, of Education, of the State
>
> Imposition – on the Family, on the Nation, on Humanity

Consequently the order to enforce practically the D...M...J... Nevertheless means.

"By every means, whatever they may be, one must Impose first on the Family, and then on the Nation in order to achieve the aim, of imposing on Humanity.

1. Destruction of Supernaturalism, there where the conscience has been read by Masonic Materialism.
2. The Destruction of Authority, there where Education has not been reached by Masonic Materialism.
3. The Destruction of Anti-Masonry, there where the state has not been reached by Masonic Materialism.

SOCIÉTÉ BIBLIQUE CANADIENNE
CANADIAN BIBLE SOCIETY
SIÈGE SOCIAL/NATIONAL OFFICE
10 Carnforth Road, Toronto, Ontario, Canada M4A 2S4
(416) 757-4171
Telex: 06-986766 TOR
Télégraphe—"Testaments Toronto"—Cable
William R. Russell
Secrétaire Général/General Secretary

May 7, 1985

Mr. Donald Huffman
Box 1537
Port Elgin, Ontrario
NOH 2CO

Dear Mr. Huffman;

I have given much thought and prayer — over a very long period of time — to your correspondence regarding the presidency of the Canadian Bible Society current held by the Honourable Dr. Gordon L. Bennett, CM, of Charlottetown, Prince Edward Island.

First, I want to apologize for my delay in responding. The concern you have expressed about Dr. Bennett's involvement in Scottish Rite Freemasonry is not a matter to be dealt with lightly; I have taken the time and opportunity to speak to many people, both within the Society and without, about a proper response to the issue you have raised. In addition, I have been involved in an unusually heavy schedule of travel — both across Canada and abroad — on behalf of the Canadian Bible Society; and my correspondence has accumulated alarmingly during my absences. Please accept my sincere apologies.

Second, I need to make clear that the presidency of the Canadian Bible Society, while symbolically that of the national leader of the organization, is in fact a largely honorary and titular position. Dr. Bennett would be the first to admit that, while he is kept well- informed about the on-going programmes, policies and problems affecting the day-to-day operations of the Society, his actual influence upon those operations is largely confined to the chairing of a few sessions of our annual general meeting held each April and the signing of various legal documents and presentation certificates.

Third, I hope to be able to do justice to the devotion and distinction with which Dr. Bennett has served not only the Canadian Bible Society, but also his denomination (the United Church of Canada), his community, his province and his nation over a lifetime. His record of public service, of private generosity and of personal commitment to our Lord Jesus Christ is well known and highly regarded by all who have dealings with him. I believe that I can safely say that the Bible cause has no better friend in Canada than Gordon Bennett.

.../2

/27

Mr. Donald Huffman
May 7, 1985
Page 2

Fourth, I have to cite the world-wide spirit of the Bible Society movement over the past 180 years, as presently exemplified by the ministries of the United Bible Societies, of which our own Canadian Bible Society was a founding and is still a constituent member. That spirit is one of inclusiveness rather than of exclusiveness — of embracing Christians of all denominations and traditions and walks who love the Word of God and who work and give and pray for its translation, publication and distribution to the peoples of the world in languages they can read and at prices they can afford. Inclusiveness is not always easy to define, let alone to discipline, and sometimes even to defend. But it is fundamental to the spiritual and material success of the Bible Society movement all over the world that we "judge not", but accept as faithful, sincere and positive the contribution of time, energy, abilities and resources of all Christians of good-will who associate themselves with our Society.

Although opposition to freemasonry is deeply felt by some Christian individuals and groups — and has been the subject of some sensational journalism recently — among other Christian traditions involvement in masonic orders is thought to be quite acceptable, even admirable. Over the twenty years of my own Presbyterian pastorates, I found that many of my most dedicated elders, best informed Church School teachers, and most generous contributors were, in fact, masons: my congregations would have been sadly impoverished had they been excluded!

For many such Christians, as certainly for Dr. Bennett, there is no sense of conflict or compromise in being a member of a masonic order and being a supporter — even a leader — of the Canadian Bible Society. The Society's mandate is clear, simple, broad and ecumenical: to translate, publish and distribute the Scriptures, and to raise funds to finance these programmes, are undertakings neither doctrinal nor denominational.

I trust — and pray — that your own on-going support of the Bible Society's mandate and ministry will be similarly open-hearted and open-handed. The service of God's Word invites — no, requires — the dynamism, the generosity, the inclusion of believers from every shade in the very wide spectrum of Canadian Christendom. I hope that the Society — and the service of the Word of God — can still count on you.

Yours faithfully,

William R. Russell
General Secretary

WRR:rj

/28

Clifton Park United Methodist Church

P.O. Box 135, Clifton Park, NY 12065-0135
(518) 371-3862

Rt 146

Rt 9

July 17, 1985

Mr. Donald Huffman
Box 1537
Port Elgin, Ont. NOH 2CO

Dear Don,

It is great being a **former** Grand Chaplain! God has been blessing beyond belief! He has given me a new boldness to proclaim His Word. I have been given the courage and Grace to fly in the face of United Methodist oppostion as indicated in the enclosed clippings.

I think I told you that I had planned to go to Texas to be a part of a national team to expose masonry. After much prayer, I felt strong led in other directions. Among the new direction was to write the forward for your new book, "Freemasonry—A Critical Bibliography". I would appreciate a copy when it become available. In addition, I have been led to prepare a message for my pulpit and congregation. I don't have a delivery date from the Lord yet, but I am prepared and willing to be used at the proper time. Perhaps the message is for others as well.

I am supposed to be on vacation during August but the Sunday that I was to be in Texas, August 11, keeps getting filled and unfilled. It may be that I am to preach this message on that Sunday. Even a vacation will not prevent me from doing it if God leads!

Thank you for bringing Charles G. Finney's message back into print. It is powerful. I would like five more copies and will request five more as funds are available. **A check for $50.00 is enclosed!**

A member of the Eastern Star came to the communion rail at our last communion service. I couldn't stand to look at her ring and couldn't refuse her the sacrament. I did pause to gently turn her ring so that it looked like a wedding band. It provided her a loud message from the look on her face.

The real purpose of this letter is to ask you, **"Please, pray with me for the delivery of this message!"** I know that God will move. Let those who have ears to hear, hear!

God bless you in your wonderful ministry.

Joyously in His Service!

Harmon R. Taylor

HARMON R. TAYLOR
pastor

HARMON R. TAYLOR, Pastor—17 Marco Polo Drive, Latham, NY 12110 (518) 783-6575

HRT MINISTRIES BOX 12, NEWTONVILLE, NY 12128-0012

May 17, 1986

Dr. Gordon L. Bennett
14 Charlotte Drive
Charlottetown, PEI
CIA 2N5 CANADA

Dear Dr. Bennett,

I entered Freemasonry as an Entered Apprentice in 1973. In 1980 I was elected Master of my Lodge receiving the Master of the Year Award for increasing Lodge attendance by 259% over the previous year. In 1983-84 I was appointed Grand Chaplain of the Grand Lodge of Free and Accepted Masons of the State of New York.

I tell you this so that you will know of my devotion to Freemasonry while a pastor in my local church. On November 25, 1984 I fled its ranks because a Christian brother had the courage to reveal to me the secrets of the Fraternity that are kept from Masons. What Masonry doesn't tell Masons are the real secrets.

I understand you are President of the Canadian Bible Society and also Lt. Grand Commander 33°. **Did you know that Albert Pike 33°, author of Morals & Dogma, a classic recommended by most Grand Lodges for study, also is credited with rewriting the Scottish Rite Ritual that it used in most jurisdictions?** Listen to what he said to the 23rd Supreme Council of the World as he addressed them as their newly installed head on July 4, 1889:

> ...that which we say to the crowd is---we **worship** a God, but it is a God that one adores without superstition. To you, Sovereign Grand Inspectors General, we say this, that you may repeat it to the Brethren of the 32nd, 31st, and 30th degrees--- **The Masonic religion should be, by all of us initiates of the high degrees, maintained in the purity of the Luciferian doctrine.** If Lucifer were not God, would Adonay (the God of the Christians) whose deeds prove his cruelty, perfidy, and hatred of man, barbarism and repulsion of Science, would Adonay and his Priests calumniate him? **Yes, Lucifer is God, and unfortunately Adonay is also God.** For the eternal law is that there is no light without shade, no beauty without ugliness, no white without black, for the absolute can only exist as two gods...Thus the doctrine of Satanism is a heresy, and the true and pure philosophic religion is the belief in Lucifer, the equal with Adonay; but **Lucifer, God of Light and God of Good, is struggling for humanity against Adonay, the God of Darkness and Evil."**

You may read this for yourself on page 220 of Occult Theocracy.

Dear Christian brother, how can any Christian remain in such an organization when faced with these facts? **I plead with you to renounce Freemasonry at once and give them your testimony for Jesus Christist.** If you will not, **then renounce Christianity and resign your post as President of the Canadian Bible Society.**

Check out the truth that the Bible is but **one of many** Volumes of Sacred Law having no more or less value than the Koran or the Book of Mormon. **Is not the Holy Bible, THE Word of God of more value than all these?** If not, why to you remain an instant as head of an organization that promotes the Bible as the Word of God.

In Christian Love,

HARMON R. TAYLOR, Pastor

The love of Christ compels us... (II Corinthians 5:14)

5

SECRET CHAMBERS

> Then said He to me, Son of man, have you seen what the Elders of the house of Israel do in the dark, every man in his (secret) chambers of (idol) pictures? For they say, The Lord does not see us; the Lord has forsaken the land. (Ezekiel 8:12)

The seventy men in the temple were not ordinary members of the public at large. They were the Elders of the people including men like Jaazaniah, the son of Shaphan (the scribe). What the Elders were worshipping, was something in secret that neither the public would be knowledgeable about and even thought the Lord may not know: "For they say, The Lord does not see us." I quote Edmond Ronayne in his extensive, comprehensive and excellent book called *The Master's Carpet or Masonry and Baal Worship Identical.* – pg. 225-227, 244, 253, 254

Preparation of Candidate in E. A. Degree. Preparation of Candidate of F. C. Degree. Preparation of Candidate in M. M. Degree.

The above engravings represent as correctly as can be, the manner of preparing candidates for the Masonic mysteries, and it will be observed in relation thereto that four conditions must always be complied with. First, the candidate must be *initiated in darkness*; second, he must be *invested with a girdle or cable-tow;* third, he must be *neither naked nor clad;* and fourth, he must be *either barefoot*, or else "*neither barefoot nor shod.*" Now what is the meaning of this singular proceeding, and why is it that there can be no deviation from this strange usage? Where did Freemasonry find these "preparation" ceremonies, and what authority is there for their adoption and continued use in all Masonic lodges?

They were all borrowed by the "Masonic fathers" from the old Baal worship of the "Ancient Mysteries," as the following authoritative teaching of Masonry will abundantly testify. We shall examine each one in the order in which they are here enumerated, beginning with the "hoodwink" or

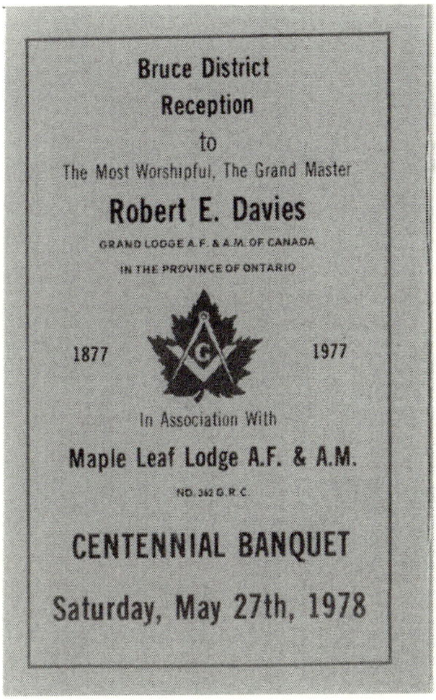
Bruce District
Reception
to
The Most Worshipful, The Grand Master
Robert E. Davies
GRAND LODGE A.F. & A.M. OF CANADA
IN THE PROVINCE OF ONTARIO
1877 1977
In Association With
Maple Leaf Lodge A.F. & A.M.
NO. 362 G.R.C.
CENTENNIAL BANQUET
Saturday, May 27th, 1978

GRAND MASTER
MOST WORSHIPFUL BROTHER ROBERT E. DAVIES
MOUNT FOREST, ONTARIO

While polytheism, or the worship of many gods, was the universal religion of the multitudes or the common people in all pagan nations, yet the sun or Sun-God, under different appellations was everywhere constituted as the chief deity. And while the pagan masses offered their public devotions to their myriads of senseless idols, the pagan priests and philosophers and rulers had a different worship, which they practiced only in secret, which they conducted with the most imposing ceremonies, and which they always celebrated in honour of the chief deity, or sun-god This secret worship of paganism in every country was termed the "Mysteries," and is that which was revived by the "Masonic fathers" in the beginning of the eighteenth century; so that what was called the "Mysteries" of Osiris, or Baal, or Bacchus, or Dionysius in ancient times, is today known as the mysteries of Masonry. On this point all our Masonic writers, as had been already mentioned, give such plain, positive, unqualified, affirmative testimony, that, if we do not believe what they say concerning their own pet philosophy, it is useless to receive human testimony on any subject. And for the purpose of illustrating this Baal worship, and as if to give emphasis to their teaching, the emblem of the sun, moon, stars, &c., on the preceding page, is found in all our lodges and manuals.

In the *Lexicon of Freemasonry*, by Mackey (insert publication date here), we read:

> Egyptian Mysteries – Egypt was the cradle of the mysteries of paganism. At one time in possession of all the learning and religion that was to be found in the world, it extended into other nations the influence of its sacred rites, and its secret doctrines. (125)

And in describing the "Mysteries," Dr. Mackey again says:

> This is the name given to those religious assemblies of the ancients, whose ceremonies were conducted in Secret, whose doctrines were known only to those who had obtained the right of knowledge by a previous initiation, and whose members were in possession of signs and tokens, by which they were enabled to recognize each other. (315)

Is not this an exact description of Freemasonry? Or could any language be employed to portray the Masonic system more accurately? But again:

> Warburton's definition of the "Mysteries was as follows. Each of the pagan gods had (besides the public and open) a secret worship paid unto him, to which none were admitted but those who had been selected by preparatory ceremonies called

> Initiation. This secret worship was termed the mysteries." (Divine Legation, vol. i, p.189.)

The most important of the mysteries were those of Mithras, celebrated in Persia; of Osiris and Isis, celebrated in Egypt; of Eleusis, instituted in Greece, and the Scandinavian and Druidical rites which were confined to the Gothic and Celtic tribes. The explanation, therefore, which Freemasonry offers for holding its lodge meetings in the upper rooms of buildings, is given as follows in the *General Ahiman Rezon*, by Sickles (publication date), we read: "Lodge meetings at the present day are usually held in upper chambers," and the reason for this custom is, that "Before the erection of temples the celestial bodies were worshipped on hills and the terrestrial ones in valleys." (75) The only reason, therefore, according to Masonic teaching, why lodge meetings are usually held in "upper chambers," is because in ancient times, *sabaism*, or the worship of the heavenly bodies, was conducted on high hills, or, as the Scriptures call them, "high places." And as very clearly explaining the term Baal and this ancient custom of worshipping on high hills as well as the consequent reason for the elevated position of our lodges in modern times, the following extract from the *Bible Cyclopaedia* may be profitably quoted. The Writer says:

> Originally Baal was the god of the sun, the ruler and vivifier of nature, and Astarte, the goddess of the moon. In the later star-worship of the Western Asiatic nations, Baal was the name of Jupiter, the planet of fate, or, as some suppose, of Saturn. The proper Phoenician name, however, of Baal was Melkart, Melkrat, or Melchrat, which is usually supposed to mean 'King of the city,' i.e. Tyre, but others consider it a contraction of two words signifying 'King of the earth.'

In Freemasonry, he is called and worshipped as the "Supreme Ruler of the Universe – the Great Architect of the Universe," &c.

"Baal was, perhaps, the same god as the Phoenician Moloch. The Greeks, for the purpose of distinction, termed him the 'Tyrian Hercules.' (Freemasonry calls him the 'Tyrian Architect.')

Again, Ezekiel 8:12 says, "Son of man, have you seen what the elders do in the dark..?"

Preparation of Candidate in E. A. Degree. Preparation of Candidate of F. C. Degree. Preparation of Candidate in M. M. Degree.

The above engravings represent as correctly as can be, the manner of preparing candidates for the Masonic mysteries, and it will be observed in relation thereto that four conditions must always be complied with. First, the candidate must be initiated in darkness; second, he must be invested with a girdle or cable-tow; third, he must be neither naked nor clad' and fourth, he must be barefoot, or else "neither barefoot nor shod." Now what is the meaning of this singular proceeding, and why is it that there can be no deviation from this strange usage? Where did Freemasonry find these "preparation" ceremonies, and what authority is there for their adoption and continued use in all Masonic lodges? They were all borrowed by the "Masonic fathers' from the old Baal worship of the "Ancient Mysteries," as the following authoritative teaching of Masonry will abundantly testify. We shall examine each one in the order in which they are here enumerated, beginning with the "hoodwink".

INITIATION IN DARKNESS

> On this head we read in the *Manual of the Lodge*, by Mackey:
>
> In the Ancient Mysteries (or sacred worship of the pagan gods) the aspirant (or candidate) was always kept for a certain period in a condition of darkness. Hence darkness became the symbol of initiation. (38)
>
> Again, in Pierson's *Traditions of Freemasonry*:
>
> In every country under heaven the Initiations were performed in caverns, either natural or artificial, and darkness was honoured with peculiar marks of veneration, by reason of its supposed priority of existence. (31)
>
> Pierson, again:
>
> The candidate has represented man when he had sunken from his original estate and like the rough ashler is unfit to form a part of the spiritual temple. He maintained the same character in the

> Mysteries. Emphatically a profane, enveloped in darkness, poor and destitute of spiritual knowledge and emblematically naked. The material darkness which is produced by the Hoodwink is an emblem of the darkness of his soul. (39)

Everywhere the "Mysteries" is the model of Masonry because candidates were initiated "in a condition of darkness," in "the secret worship of the pagan gods." So candidates are initiated "in a condition of darkness" in the mysteries of Masonry, and hence a hoodwink must be used. In the *Symbolism of Freemasonry*, by Mackey, we read:

> In all the ancient systems of initiation, (into the Mysteries) the candidate was shrouded in darkness as a preparation for the reception of light. Celtic mysteries of Druidism, the period in which the aspirant was immersed in darkness was nine days and nights; among the Greeks at Eleusis it was three times as long and in the still severer rites of Mithras in Persia, fifty days of darkness, solitude and fasting were imposed upon the adventurous neophyte, who by these excessive trials was at length entitled to the full communication of the light of knowledge. (155)
>
> Mackey adds, "Darkness was the symbol of initiation." (136)

The duration of darkness in the Masonic Mysteries, or in the revived form of these old pagan systems, is not quite so severe. The Entered Apprentice is hoodwinked for about the space of an hour; the Fellow Craft for about an hour and a half, while the Master Mason, in the greater, or Sublime Mysteries of Osiris, is compelled to remain in darkness for at least three hours. And lest any connecting link in the wonderful chain of evidence, binding the "Mysteries of Masonry" and the "Mysteries of Baal" together, might be wanting, the reason why lodge meetings are always held in the night time, is stated as follows in the *Symbolism of Freemasonry*, by Mackey:

> Darkness like death is the symbol of initiation. It was for this reason that all the ancient initiations were performed at night. The celebration of the mysteries was always nocturnal. The same custom prevails in Freemasonry and the explanation is the same. (157)

This language is so plain that it needs no comment. Because the Osirian Mysteries were celebrated at night, so the Masonic Mysteries must in like manner, be celebrated at night. Again, in the *History of Initiation*, by Dr. Oliver, other than whom a greater Masonic writer has never lived, we read:

> There was also another quality of the mind, which served to recommend the Mysteries, that strange attachment to the marvellous, by which every grade of human nature is swayed. To excite this sentiment in all its sublimity of horror, the initiations were performed at the dead of night. (19)

DURING THE RITUAL OF THE FIRST THREE DEGREES IN MASONRY

The three "ruffians" then propose once to make their escape; Typhon, or night and darkness, to all appearance has now completely triumphed. Osiris or Baal—the "fertilizing and fecundating power of the sun"—is now apparently buried out of sight, the lodge becomes a house of mourning, and Isis or nature weeps for the loss of her husband. Referring to this melancholy scene and at the same time conclusively proving what has been already stated, that the so-called "higher degrees" are but so many developments of the "Sublime degree of Master Mason," we read as follows in the *Book of the Ancient and Accepted Scottish Rite*:

> M...P...- "My brethren, the power of darkness has prevailed over the prince of light. The earth mourns and is wrinkled with frost. All nature laments, and we share the common sorrow. Excellent Senior Warden, let prayers be offered up in the tabernacle for the return of light and the re-ascension of the Sun.
>
> Senior Warden: - Most Puissant, our ancient taskmasters on the banks of the Nile mourn for Osiris. The Chaldeans lament for Bel (or Baal) and the Phoenicians for Tammuz. The Phrygian women clash their cymbals and weep for Atys; while far in India the Brahmins pray for the return of Cama."
>
> M...P...- We, like our ancient Masters weep for Osiris – the type to us of the sun, of light, of life. Weep, my brethren, for Osiris! Weep for light lost, and life departed, and the good and the beautiful oppressed by evil." (355-56)

6

WOMEN WEEPING FOR TAMMUZ (OSIRIS)

Ezekiel says:

> He also said to me, yet again you shall see greater abominations which they are committing. Then He brought me to the entrance of the north gate of the Lord's house; and behold, there sat women weeping for Tammuz. (A Babylonian god who was supposed to die annually and subsequently be resurrected). (8:13-14)

In all the Ancient Mysteries, there was essentially a trinity—God the father/husband, goddess the mother, and god the child. God the father or husband was worshipped under various names in the various Mysteries. Tammuz was the same as Bacchus (with the Phoenicians), the same as Adonis (to the Phrygians), the same as Osiris (in Egypt), the same as "Hiram Abiff" in Freemasonry! The following is taken from Rev. Alexander Hislop's book, *The Two Babylons* pg. 21, 55-60, and 67-69:-

Sub-Section I. – The Child in Assyria,

The original of that mother, so widely worshipped, there is reason to believe, was Seminamis, already referred to, who, it is well known was worshipped by the Babylonians, and other eastern nations, and that under the name of Rhea, the great Goddess "Mother."

It was from the son, however, that she derived all her glory and her claims to deification. That son, though represented as a child in his mother's arms, was a person of great stature and immense bodily powers, as well as most fascinating manners. In Scripture he is referred to (Ezek. Viii. 14) under the name of Tammuz, but he is commonly known among classical writers under the name of Bacchus, that is, "The Lamented One."

From Bakhah "to weep" or "lament." Among the Phoenicians, says Hesychius, "Bacchos means weeping," p. 179. As the women wept for Tammus, so did they for Bacchus. Page 21

Sub Section IV. – The Death of the Child

The identity of Nimrod, however, and the Egyptian Osiris, having been established, we have thereby light as to Nimrod's death. Osiris met with a violent death, and that violent death of Osiris was the central theme of the whole idolatry of Egypt. If Osiris was Nimrod, as we have seen, that violent death which the Egyptians so pathetically deplored in their annual festivals was just the death of Nimrod. The accounts in regard to the death of the god worshipped in the several mysteries of the different countries are all to the same effect. A statement of Plato seems to show, that in his day the Egyptian Osiris was regarded as identical with Tammuz; and Tammuz is well known to have been the same as Adonis, the famous Huntsman, for whose death Venus is fabled to have made such bitter lamentations. As the women of Egypt wept for Osiris, as the Phoenician and Assyrian women wept for Tammuz, so in Greece and Rome the women wept for Baccus, whose name, as we have seen, means "The bewailed," or "Lamented One." And now in connection with the Bacchanal lamentations, the importance of the relation established between Nebros, "The spotted fawn," and Nebrod, "The mighty hunter," will appear. The Nebros, or "Spotted fawn," was the symbol of Bacchus, as representing Nebrod or Nimrod himself. Now, on certain occasions, in the mystical celebrations, the Nebros, or "spotted fawn," was torn in pieces, expressly, as we learn from Photius, as a commemoration of what happened to Bacchus, whom that fawn represented. The tearing in pieces of Nebros, "the spotted one," goes to confirm the conclusion, that the death of Bacchus, even as the death of Osiris, represented the death of Nebrod, whom, under the very name of "The Spotted one," the Babylonians worshipped. Page 55 – 58.

Sub-Section V. – The Deification of the Child

If there was one who was more deeply concerned in the tragic death of Nimrod than another, it was his wife Semiramis, who, from an originally humble position, had been raised to share with him the throne of Babylon. What, in this emergency shall she do? Shall she quietly forego the pomp and pride which she has been raised? No. Though the death of her husband has given a rude shock to her power, yet her resolution and unbounded ambition were nowise checked. On the contrary, her ambition took a still higher flight. In life her husband had been honoured as a hero; in death she will have him worshipped as a god, yea, as the woman's promised seed, "Zero-ashta," *who was destined to bruise the serpent's head, and who in doing so, was to have his own heel bruised. The patriarchs, and the ancient world in general, were perfectly acquainted with the grand primeval promise of Eden, and they knew right well that the bruising of the heel of the promised seed implied his death, and that the curse could be removed from the world only by the death of the grand Deliverer. If the promise about the bruising of the serpent's head, recorded in Genesis, as made to our first parents, *Zero – in Chaldee, "the seed."

(It is equally clear also in stating that he perished by a violent death, even as was the case with Nimrod, Tammuz, or Bacchus).

Was actually made, and if all mankind were descended from them, then it might be expected that some trace of this promise would be found in all nations. And such is the fact. There is hardly a people or kindred on earth in whose mythology it is not shadowed forth. The Greeks represented their great god Apollo as slaying the serpent Pytho, and Hercules as strangling serpents while yet in his cradle. In Egypt, in India, in Scandinavia, in Mexico, we find clear allusions to the same great truth. "The evil genius," says Wilkinson, "of the adversaries of the Egyptian god Horus is frequently figured under the form of a snake, whose head he is seen piercing with a spear. The same fable occurs in the religion of India, where the malignant serpent Calyia is slain by Vishnu, in his avatar of Crishna (Fig. 23); and the Scandinavian deity Thor was said to have bruised the head of the great serpent with his mace."

After the candidates for initiation had passed through the confessional, and swore the required oaths, "strange and amazing objects," says Wilkinson, "presented themselves. Sometimes the place they were in seemed to shake around them; sometimes it appeared bright and resplendent with light and radian fire, and then again covered with black darkness, sometimes thunder and lightning sometimes frightful noises and bellowing, sometimes terrible apparitions astonished the trembling spectators." Then, at last, the great god, the central object of their worship, Osiris, Tammus, Nimrod or Adonis, was revealed to them in the way most fitted to soothe their feelings and engage their blind affections. An account of such a manifestation is thus given by an ancient Pagan, cautiously indeed, but yet in such a way as shows the nature of the magic secret by which such an apparent miracle was accomplished:

"In a manifestation which one must not reveal...there is seen on a wall of the temple a mass of light, which appears at first at a very great distance. It is transformed, while unfolding itself, into a visage evidently divine and supernatural, of an aspect severe, but with a touch of sweetness. Following the teachings of a mysterious religion, the Alexandrians honour it as Osiris or Adonis." From the light reflected on Babylon by Egypt, as well as from the form of the extant images of the Babylonian child in the arms of the goddess-mother, we have every reason to believe that this was actually done. In Egypt the fair Horus, the son of the black Osiris, who was the favourite object of worship, in the arms of the goddess Isis, was said to have been miraculously born in consequence of a connection, on the part of that goddess, with Osiris after his death, and, in point of fact, to have been a new incarnation of that god, to avenge his death on his murderers. Pages 58 to 69.

The following is an excerpt from *The Masonic Report* on the Masonic Legend/Ritual of "Hiram Abiff" by Cecil F. McQuaig: pg. 28, 29:

4. Question: Is it possible to make a parallel comparison of the legends of Hiram and Osiris?

Answer: Absolutely!

In the Egyptian legend of Osiris we notice the following principle details:

1. A valuable thing is possessed by Osiris – a kingdom.
2. There is conspiracy – by Typhon and his Fellows.
3. There is a conflict – Typhon and his fellows had a conflict with Osiris.
4. There is a death – Osiris is slain by Typhon.
5. The death is by the hand of a brother, Osiris is slain by Typhon.

6. The body is buried at the foot of a tamarind tree.
7. There is a first search – Isis searches for her husband's body.
8. She interrogates everyone whom she meets.
9. The search is accidentally successful – Isis finds the body and disposes of it.
10. There is a second search. Isis searches for the scattered parts of the body of Osiris a second time.
11. There is another finding – Isis finds all the parts of the body but one.
12. There is a loss – One part of the body is missing.
13. There is a substitution – Isis substitutes the Phallus for the missing part.

In the Masonic legend of Hiram Abiff we may notice the principle details and compare:

1. A valuable thing is possessed by Hiram – the Master's word.
2. There is a conspiracy – Twelve Fellow Crafts conspire against Hiram Abiff.
3. There is a conflict – Three ruffians attack Hiram Abiff at high twelve.
4. There is a death – Hiram is slain by Jubelum.
5. This death is by the hand of a brother – Hiram is slain by his brother Mason, Jubelum.
6. The body is buried at the foot of a tamarind or acacia tree.
7. There is a first search – the Fellow Crafts search for the ruffians.
8. They interrogate everyone whom they meet.
9. This search is accidentally successful – The ruffians are found and disposed of.
10. There is a second search – three Fellow Crafts go in search of the body.

11. There is another finding – The body of Hiram is found in a grave dug due east and west.
12. here is a loss – The Master's word is missing.
13. There is a substitution – The first word spoken after the body is raised is substituted by Solomon.

Thus we discover that even in the most detail the Masonic legend of Hiram Abiff and the old legend of Osiris are one and the same, the only difference being that the name of Osiris was dropped by the "Masonic Fathers" and the name of Hiram Abiff, a name that the Princes of Masonry know is not accurate or proper, was substituted in its place. (See Pike's "Morals and Dogma," p. 79). The "Master's Word is symbolic; it symbolizes the generative organ "Phallus" of the Egyptian legend.

5. Question: Is there further proof that the sun-god of Egypt's religion and the sun-god of Freemasonry's religion are one and the same?

Answer: Yes! In the "Traditions of Freemasonry," by Past Grand Master Pierson, p. 240, we read: "The Masonic legend stands by itself, unsupported by history or other than its own traditions: yet we readily recognize in Hiram Abiff the Osiris of the Egyptians, the Mithras of the Persians, the Bacchus of the Greeks, the Dionysius of the fraternity of the artificers, the Atys of the Phrygians, whose passion, death and resurrection were celebrated by these people respectively."

6. Question: Now that we have seen again that Osiris and Hiram Abiff are one and the same; we ask, who was Osiris, and what did he actually represent?

Answer: In the "Lexicon of Freemasonry," by Albert G. Mackey, p. 130, we read as follows: "This legend was purely astronomical. Osiris was the sun, Isis the moon. Typhon was the symbol of winter, which destroys the fecundating and fertilizing power of the sun, thus as it were, depriving him of life.

This was the catastrophe celebrated in the mysteries, and the aspirant (candidate) was made to pass fictitiously through the sufferings and death of Osiris." To which we could add, just as the candidate in the third degree does in his impersonation of Hiram Abiff.

7. Question: Is Freemasonry a modern form of primitive sun-worship?

Answer: In the "Traditions of Freemasonry," by Pierson, p. 34, this question of Masonic sun-worship is placed beyond the possibility of doubt. Pierson: "Baxot tells us in his Manuel de Franc Macon, - French Manual of Free Masonry – p. 154, that the veneration which Masons entertain for the east confirms an opinion previously announced, that the religious system of Masonry comes from the east, and has reference to the primitive religion whose first occupation was the worship of the sun."

8. Question: Is Hiram Abiff Freemasonry's substitute for Jesus Christ?

Answer: Yes! In "Mystic Masonry," by Daniel Sickles, p. 248, we read: "Few candidates may be aware that Hiram whom they have represented and personified is ideally and precisely the same as Christ. Yet such is undoubtedly the case."

NOTE:- Concerning the significance of "Facing the East" and "Tammuz" here are some comments and explanations on the rituals of the first three degrees in Masonry from Edmond Ronayne's book "The Master's Carpet (Mah-Hah-Bone)" pg. 371-373, 381-383:-

In the mysteries of Osiris, the substitute was called Phallus, in the mysteries of Hiram; it is called Mah-hah-bone. And as "the Point within a Circle" represents the Phallus and as it also, as we previously learned, represents the Worshipful Master, and lastly as the Worshipful Master represents the sun-god rising in the east, therefore it undoubtedly follows that Mah-hah-bone is the real name of the god of Masonry, the "G. A.O.T.U." of its worship, which Freemasons are always to pronounce "with awe and reverence," and which, in fact, they were solemnly (?) sworn never to speak above their breath, and even then only "upon the five points of fellowship." And this being unquestionably the case, the religion of Masonry ought in all consistency to be called the "Mysteries of Mah-hah-bone," as the religion of Egypt was anciently called the "Mysteries of Osiris."

You ask can a man be a Mason and a Christian. My dear sir, answer your own question, can this man – this minister-lying here on the lodge room floor be a Christian? He is undoubtedly a sworn worshipper of Baal, for in fact he is just now representing the Baal or Tammuz of the "Ancient Mysteries." Tell me then, through all his initiatory ceremonies thus far and more especially in his present position, can you say that he is a follower of the Lord Jesus Christ?

You ask can a man be a Mason and a Christian? My dear sir, answer your own question, can this man—this minister—lying here on the lodge room floor be a Christian? He is undoubtedly a sworn worshipper of Baal, for in fact he is just now representing the Baal or Tammuz of the "Ancient Mysteries." Tell me then, through all his initiatory ceremonies thus far, and more especially in his present position, can you say that he is a follower of the Lord Jesus Christ?

In Sharp's "Egyptian Mythology," p. 10, we read that:—

"The death of Osiris was piously *lamented* by Isis and her sister Nephtys; and once a year the Egyptians joined their priests in a *melancholy procession* through the streets, *singing a doleful ditty*, called the Maneros or Song of Love which was to console the goddess for the loss of her husband."

And because the Egyptian sun-worshippers "joined" their priests in a melancholy procession, "singing a doleful ditty" in commemoration of the death of Osiris, so the Masonic fraternity or the modern Baal worshippers, in imitation of their ancient brethren, join their priests in a similar procession and for precisely the same purpose.

In Sharp's *Egyptian Mythology*, we read that:

> The death of Osiris was piously lamented by Isis and her sister Nephtys; and once a year the Egyptians joined their priests in a melancholy procession through the streets, singing a doleful ditty, called the Maneros or Song of Love which was to console the goddess for the loss of her husband. (10)

Because the Egyptian sun-worshippers "joined" their priests in a melancholy procession, "singing a doleful ditty" in commemoration of the death of Osiris, so the Masonic fraternity or the modern Baal worshippers, in imitation of their ancient brethren, join their priests in a similar procession and for precisely the same purpose. This is the same death and resurrection so graphically represented in the Master Mason's degree by the pretended death and burial of the candidate, and his subsequent raising by the "paw of the lion," and the god recognized in this Pagan philosophy the god of nature, or the fecundating power of the sun-is the god to whom prayers are offered in Masonic worship. The names given to this fictitious deity, as has been already explained, were different in different countries, so that the Baal of Samaria was the Osiris of Egypt, and is unquestionably the Hiram of Masonry. In the eighth chapter of Ezekiel this idol is designated by the name of Tammuz, and, as we shall see hereafter, is the self-same deity whom every Mason, minister, as well as rum-seller, must personate in the sublime mysteries of the third degree.

TAMMUZ—IDENTICAL WITH HIRAM—HIS SECRET WORSHIP REVEALED TO EZEKIEL

> Then he brought me to the door of the gate of the Lord's house, which was toward the north, and behold there sat women weeping for Tammuz. (Ezekiel 8:14)

Now, who was this Tammuz? What did he represent, if anything? And what is meant by "women weeping" for him? You will remember, my dear Henry, that it has been demonstrated over and over again as clearly as possible that the Osiris of the old Egyptians Mysteries and the Hiram of modern Freemasonry are one and the same; also, that Osiris and Adonis were but different names applied by people of different countries to the same principle – the sun-god, or "the fecundating and fertilizing powers of nature." Now, let us examine what Freemasonry has to say concerning Tammuz and his identity with the hero-god or the Baal of the old Pagan Mysteries. In the *Lexicon of Freemasonry* by Mackey, I read:

> Adonis, Mysteries of: The Mysteries, which consecrated to Osiris in passing over into Phoenician were dedicated to Adonis. Adonis, in the Phoenician language, like Adon, in the Cognate Hebrew, signifies Lord or Master. The Idol Tammuz, mentioned in the eight chapter of Ezekiel, was considered by Jerome, and after him by Parkhurst, as identical with Adonis. (19)

Again, in the *Symbolism of Freemasonry*:

> In the mythology of the philosophers Adonis was a symbol of the sun, but his death by violence, and his subsequent restoration to life, made him the analogue of Hiram Abiff in the Masonic system and identify the spirit of the initiation in his

> Mysteries, which was to teach the second life with that of the third degree of Freemasonry. (3-4)

From all this testimony, then, which could be easily multiplied, you will at once perceive that Tammuz and Adonis are identical, and inasmuch as Hiram, Osiris and Adonis are also identical, therefore, it unquestionably follows that the Hiram of the Master Mason's degree is precisely the same character as that formerly worshipped by the wicked and rebellious Jews under the name of Tammuz. We have yet a fuller explanation concerning the worship of this idol, the lamentation made for him by the women of Judah, and his absolute identity with the Baal of Ahab's time in Godwyn's *Moses and Aaron*, as follows:

> The sun was also worshipped by the house of Judah under the name of Tammuz, for Tammuz, saith Hierom, was Adonis, and Adonis is generally interpreted the sun, from the Hebrew word Adan, signifying dominus, the same as Baal, or Moloch, formerly did the lord or prince of the planets. The month which we call June, was by the Hebrews called Tammuz; and the entrance of the sun into the sign cancer was in Jews' astronomy termed Tekupha Tammuz, the revolution of Tammuz. About the time of our Saviour, the Jews held it unlawful to pronounce that essential name of God, Jehovah; and instead thereof, read Adonai, to prevent the heathen blaspheming that holy name by the adoption of the name Jove, etc, to the idols. Concerning Adonis, whom some ancient writers call Osiris, there are two things remarkable. The death, or loss of Adonis, and the finding of him again; as there was great lamentation at his loss, so was there great joy at his finding. By the death or

> loss of Adonis, we are to understand the departure of the sun; by his finding again, the return of that luminary. How he seemeth to depart twice in the year; first, when he is in the tropic of cancer, in the farthest degree northward; and, secondly, when he is in the tropic of Capricorn, in the farthest degree southward. Hence, we may note, that the Egyptians celebrated their Adonai in the month of November, when the sun began to be farthest southward, and the house of Judah there in the months of June, when the sun was farthest northward; yet both were for the same reasons. Some authors say that this lamentation was performed over an image in the night season; and when they had sufficiently lamented, a candle was brought into the room, which ceremony might mystically denote the return of the sun, then the priest, with a soft voice, muttered these words, 'Trust ye in God, for out of pains salvation is come to us.' (page numbers)

We learn from this corroborative testimony, then, that the idolatrous Jews in Jerusalem worshipped the sun-god under the name of Tammuz, that they made an image of a man, which they laid out (on a bed of lettuce) as dead, that lamentation was made "in the night season" over this supposed dead body, and the being so represented as dead was in other countries recognized as Osiris, Baal or Adonis. In the Master Mason's degree there is precisely the same scenic representation, as we have already seen. A man is slain by violence and is laid out as dead. This tragic performance is invariably at night; the lodge room is shrouded in gloom and darkness; grief and lamentation for the loss of the hero-god is everywhere apparent, and at last, when a sufficient time has elapsed, the sun-god, or Hiram, is again restored to life, light is introduced, and in the language of Hutchinson, as in the above extract, the candidate is raised "from the grave of inequity to the faith of salvation." Thus then, there can be no question whatever as to the identity of Tammuz with the Hiram of Masonry, and neither can there be any doubt as to the absolute idolatry of Masonic worship and its positive and emphatic condemnation by the Word of God. And inasmuch as God himself not only revealed to Ezekiel the secret mysteries of the Tammuz worship, but also pronounces, in verse eighteen, a most terrible judgement on the wicked and back-slidden worshippers, so we are undoubtedly to learn from the same Scriptures that it is his divine will that the secret mysteries of Hiram should be also revealed, and that the false and idolatrous worship of that ancient idol (thought under a modern name) be forever banished from his church and from any fellowship whatever with the Gospel of Christ.

7

FACES TOWARD THE EAST

> Then said (the spirit) to me, have you seen this, O son of man" Yet again you shall see greater abominations that they are committing. And He brought me to the inner court of the Lord's house; and behold, at the door of the temple of the Lord, between the porch and the bronze altar, were about twenty-five men with their backs to the temple of the Lord and their faces toward the east, and they were bowing themselves toward the east and worshipping the sun. (Ezekiel 8:15-16)

Below, is God's divine layout for the camp of Israel in the wilderness. (Read Numbers chapter 2)

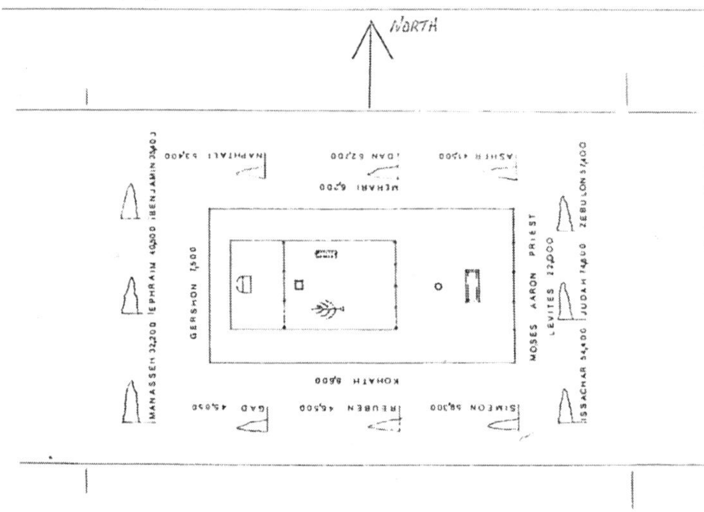

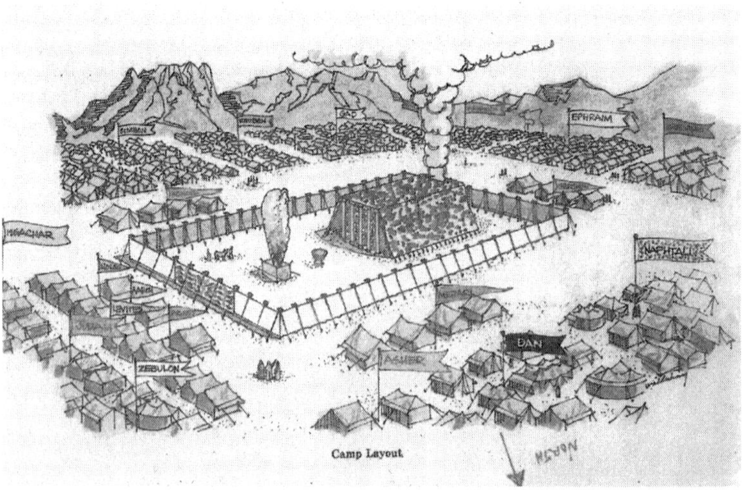

Camp Layout

The orientation of the lodges as that of the heathen temples where "the entrance was by a portico at the western front" was just the exact opposite of God's divine instruction to the building of the tabernacle in the wilderness. The Word of God says:

> Now those who camp on the east side toward the sunrise shall be of the standard of the camp of Judah ... Now those who were to camp before the tabernacle eastward, before the tent of meeting toward the sunrise ... (Numbers 2:3, 3:38)

The word Judah means "praise" (Gen. 29:35): "Enter His gates with thanks giving, and His courts with Praise." (Psalm 100:4) Instead of their faces toward God in Praise and adoration, they have their backs toward Him in the Masonic Lodge: "(and there) were about twenty-five men with their backs to the temple of the Lord and Their Faces toward the East' (Ezekiel 8:16)

The following is taken from *The Masonic Report*, by C.F. McQuaig:

1. Question: What is the local Masonic Lodge a symbol of in the Masonic philosophy?
   Answer: Albert Pike in his "Morals and Dogma," p. 209 says: "And so in our day every Masonic Lodge represents the Universe."
2. Question: In what way does the Local Masonic Lodge represent the Universe?
   Answer: From "The Master's Carpet," by Edmond Ronayne, past Grand Master of Lodge 639 in Chicago, pp. 301-302, we read: "The Lodge room then is brought before us as a symbol of the Universe, governed by the sun-god, and its cubical form expressed in the language of the ritual is made to represent the united power of light and darkness, and the constant conflict which is supposed to be always going on between them. In other words, the lodge room is the real heaven (in miniature), where the "god of nature," the G.A.O.T.U.." – always presides, where his symbol is always displayed, where his worship is always practiced, and when the "good Mason" (?) dies he

is simply transferred from his lower heaven or this "lodge below", to the Mount Olympus of the craft, called the "Grand Lodge above."

3. Question: Why does the Masonic ritual prescribe that every lodge, if at all possible, be situated due east and west? Answer: From the "Manual of the Lodge." By Albert G. Mackey, p.55 we read as follows: "The orientation of lodges or their position east and west is derived from the universal custom of antiquity. The heathen temples," says Dudley, "were so constructed that their length was directed towards the east, and the entrance was by a portico at the western front, where the altar stood so that votaries (candidates) approaching for the performance of religious rites, directed their faces toward the east, the quarter of sunrise. The primitive reason for this custom undoubtedly is to be found in the early prevalence of sun-worship, and hence the spot where that luminary (the sun) first made his appearance in the heavens was consecrated in the minds of his (the suns) worshippers as a place entitled to peculiar reverence. Freemasonry retaining in its symbolism, imperatively requires, when it can be done that the lodge should be situated due east and west, so that every ceremony shall remind the Mason of the progress of that luminary (the sun). (15, 17-19)

In the Masonic Lodge, there are a number of rites, rituals, and ceremonies the candidate is required to go through to become a completed Mason of the third degree. Namely, they are the preparation of the candidate, "Initiation in Darkness"; Initiatory Ceremonies—namely, Rite of Induction, Rite of Circumambulation, Rite of Secrecy, Rite of Illumination, Rite of Intrusting and Rite of Investiture. All of these ceremonies centre around Sun Worship, and in a number of steps in the process, before receiving the so-called "New Birth", they are Required to

Face the East! All this with a death threatening oath of secrecy before you understand what you are going through! Albert Pike, Sovereign Pontiff of Universal Freemasonry says, "Masonry, like all the religions, all the Mysteries, conceals its secrets from all except the Adepts and Sages...!"

RITE OF CIRCUMAMBULATION

The next ceremony through which the candidate is made to pass is called the "Rite of Circumambulation," or "the symbolic pilgrimage" in search of light. In the *Manual of the Lodge*, by Mackey, we read:

> The circumambulation among the pagan nations referred to the great doctrine of Sabaism, or sun-worship. Freemasonry alone has preserved the primitive meaning, which was a symbolic allusion to the sun, as the source of physical light and the most wonderful work of the "Grand Architect of the Universe.' The lodge represents the world; the three principal officers represent the sun in her three principal positions – at rising, at meridian, and at setting. The circumambulation, therefore, alludes to the apparent course of the solar orb, through these points around the world. (page number)

This proves beyond the shadow of a doubt, that Masonry is the religious philosophy of the old Baal, or sun-worshippers, revived, and that the sun-god is constantly referred to in this, as in all the other ceremonies of initiation.

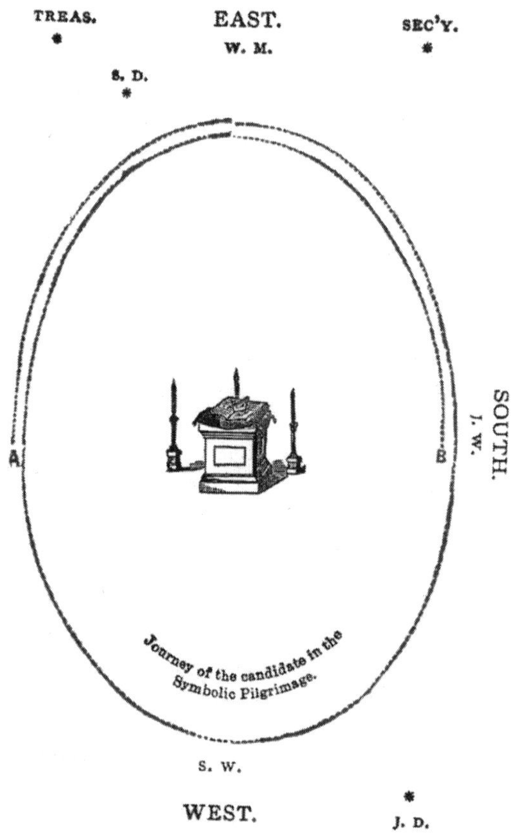

Again, in Pierson's "Traditions," p. 32:—

"In the rite of circumambulation, we find another ceremony *borrowed* from the ancient Freemasonry, that was practiced in the MYSTERIES. In ancient Greece, when the priests were engaged in the rite of sacrifice, they and the people always 'walked' three times round the altar, while singing a sacred hymn. In making this procession, great care was taken to move in imitation of the course of the sun. For this purpose, they commenced at the east, and passing by the way of the south to the west, and thence by the north, they arrived at the east again."

This is an exact description of the Masonic "rite of circumambulation," and in the absence of any further testimony, even, is sufficient of itself to establish the identity of Freemasonry, with the "Ancient Mysteries," or the "secret worship" of Baal or the sun-god.

Again, in Pierson's *Traditions*:

> In the rite of circumambulation, we find another ceremony borrowed from the ancient Freemasonry that was practiced in the Mysteries. In ancient Greece, when the priests were engaged in the rite of sacrifice, they and the people always 'walked' three times round the altar, while singing a sacred hymn. In making this procession, great care was taken to move in imitation of the course of the sun. For this purpose, they commenced at the east, and passing by the way of the south to the west, and thence by the north, they arrived at the east again. (32)

This is the exact description of the Masonic "rite of circumambulation," and in the absence of any further testimony, even, is sufficient of itself to establish the identity of Freemasonry, with the "Ancient Mysteries," or the "secret worship" of Baal or the sun-god. Again, on the same page, we read, "Among the Romans, also, the rite of circumambulation was always used in the rites of sacrifice of expiation, or purification." And again:

> Among the Hindoos, the same rite of circumambulation has always been practiced. A Brahmin, upon rising from bed in the morning, having first adored the sun, while directing his face to the East, then walks toward the West, by the way of the South, saying at the same time, 'I follow the course of the sun.' The same ceremony was in use in the Druidical rites. The priests always made three circuits from east to west, by the right hand around the altar, accompanied by all the worshippers. (33)

And, Mr. Grand Captain General Pierson, in explaining the number of revolutions to be made, and the particular line of march which the candidate must pursue, explains very clearly, the true import and the origin of this particular rite. He says in *Traditions of Freemasonry*:

> It will be well for the Masonic student, in tracing out these analogies (i.e. the analogies between Freemasonry and the Ancient Mysteries) to constantly bear in mind that in the 'rite of circumambulation' the number of revolutions may, and does vary, according to different contingencies, although, of course, the number three is most important as a mystic and sacred number, but that at all times the ceremony must be performed with the course of the sun, turning to the right, and having the altar on the right hand. (33)

This is precisely the manner, as will be seen from the above figure, in which this particular rite is performed now, and from the minute description given of it as it existed in the secret worship of Baal, it will be observed at once, how anxious our Masonic teachers are to prove that it has been revived without any material change, and that it occupies the very self-same position today in Freemasonry that it formerly did in the "Ancient Mysteries."

RITE OF SECRECY

The next ceremony demanding our attention is the rite of secrecy, which is performed in the following manner. The candidate having passed through the rite of the "symbolic pilgrimage," and having made the same public confession before the three principal officers of the lodge, in the South, West and East respectively, as he made at the door, he is ordered by the Worshipful Master, or "Chief Hierophant, "to be reconducted to the Senior Warden in the West, where he is taught how to approach the East, by one, two, or three, upright regular steps, as the case may be, and then caused to kneel at the altar in "due form." And now what is the origin of this ceremony? And why are Masonic candidates sworn, and in this peculiar manner? The *Freemason's Guide*, by Sickles, gives us the reason in the following language:

> Among the ancients – i.e. in the Mysteries – silence and secrecy were considered virtues of the highest order. The Egyptians worshipped Harpocrates, the god of secrecy, raised altars in his name, and wreathed them with garlands of flowers. Among the ancient Romans, too, these virtues were not less esteemed, and a distinguished Latin poet tells us 'for faithful silence also there is a sure reward.'(62)

Traditions of Freemasonry, by Pierson:

> An oath taken with the face toward the east – i.e. in the mysteries – was deemed more solemn and binding than when taken with the face toward any other cardinal point. (34)

RITE OF ILLUMINATION

The initiatory ceremonies of Freemasonry, in any of its degrees, might be properly divided into three separate periods: First, the period of preparation in the ante-room, concluding with the admission of the candidate into the lodge; secondly, the period of darkness and gloom, or the hoodwink period, during which, the first three religious rites of "Induction", "Circumambulation," and

"Secrecy," are performed, and lastly, the period of light embracing the three remaining ceremonies of "Illumination," "Intrusting," and "Investiture," and during which also, the pretended secrets of the order are communicated to the candidate, and the symbolic philosophy of the system is explained. The following is an excerpt from *The Masonic Report,* by C.F. McQuaig:

15. Question: In the first degree a Masonic ceremony known as the "Rite of Illumination" is conducted, in which the candidate is supposedly brought to Masonic light; what is the source of this ceremony?

Answer:: From Albert Pike's "Morals and Dogma," p. 368, we read as follows: "The Goths, had three great festivals; the most magnificent of which commenced at the winter solstice; and was celebrated in honour of Thor, the Prince of the Power of the Air. Thor was the Sun, the Egyptian Osiris and Knephk the Phoenician Bel or Baal. The initiations were had in huge intricate caverns, terminating, as all the Mithriac caverns did, in a spacious vault, where the candidate was brought to light."

16. Question: In performing "The Rite of Secrecy" the candidate must always face the east, place his hand on the square, compass and book of law, and take oaths carrying horrible penalties; was this rite borrowed from Baal worship?

Answer: In Freemasonry's "Manual of the Lodge," by Albert G. Mackey, p. 41, we read the following: "Numa was the first who erected an altar to Fides, under which name the goddess of oaths and honesty, was worshipped. Obligations taken in her name were considered as more inviolable than any other.

"And so," says Edmond Ronayne, "Freemasonry has not only "borrowed" or "revived" the rite of secrecy from the "Ancient

Mysteries" of Baal, but it has actually borrowed, and regards with religious veneration, the idol goddess, in whose name the obligations or oaths of secrecy were always administered." (Master's Carpet p. 277)

18. Questions: Do the three principle officers of the lodge: the Worshipful Master, the Senior Warden and the Junior Warden represent the movement of the sun in any way?

Answer: In the "Freemasons Guide," by Daniel Sickles, p. 66, we read as follows: "The Worshipful Master represents the sun at its rising, the Senior Warden represents the sun at its setting, and the Junior Warden represents the sun at Meridian."

And on p. 108 of "Symbolism of Freemasonry." We learn from the Indian Pantheon, "that when the sun rises in the east, he is Brahma, when he gains his meridian, he is Siva, and when he sets in the west, and he is Vishnu."

In reviewing chapter six "The Masonic Lodge and Ritual," we have learned that every officer every piece of furniture, "every ornament, emblem and fixture from the flooring to the ceiling represents some aspect of nature worship as it was practiced by those of the ancient mysteries. That the ceremonies and rituals portray some element of nature as it is centered around the sun as he makes his diurnal revolution. That the candidate himself impersonates the sun-god who is supposedly slain by darkness. The three principle officers of the lodge; the Worshipful Master, the Senior Warden and the Junior Warden represent the three stations of the sun. (17-19)

RITE OF INVESTITURE

The last rite of the Masonic initiatory ceremonies and the one which next demands our attention is called the "Rite of Investiture." The candidate having received the new birth in the rite of illumination, and having been mentally and morally enlightened through the "rite of intrusting," he is now presented with the lamb-skin, of white leather apron, and this presentation of the apron, and teaching him how to wear it, is called the "rite of investiture."

8

THEY PUT THE BRANCH TO THEIR NOSE

Then (the Spirit) said to me, have you seen this, O son of man? Is it too slight a thing to the house of Judah to commit the abominations which they commit here, that they must fill the land with violence and turn back afresh to provoke Me to anger? And behold, they put the branch to their nose (actually, before their mouths, in superstitious worship)! (Ezekiel 8:17)

The following is a section of a Masonic publication, "Short Talk Bulletin":

Short Talk Bulletin – Vol. X November, 1932 No. 11

"Finally we find in our own stately prayer in the Master's Degree, such a coupling up of a tree and life immortal; "For there is hope of a tree if it be cut down, that it will sprout again, and that the tender branches thereof will not cease." – Which of course, is taken from Job 14:7.

Thus there is ample historical recognition of the connection between that which grows and dies and grows again, and the idea of immortality; we do not have to consider the undoubted fact that "Shittah-trees" cut to form beams of house, often sprouted branches even when they had no roots, nor our own thought of almost any variety of pine as the evergreen, or ever living tree, to see that there is much background behind the symbol.

When he who was weary, plucked at a sprig of acacia, he had "evidence of things not seen." When we toss the little sprig of evergreen which is our usual cemetery "sprig of acacia" into the open grave of one of our brethren who has stepped ahead upon the path we all must tread, we give evidence of belief in a "thing not seen." For never a man has seen the spirit of one who has gone, or vision I can see the Acacia – we can look back through the dragging years to the legend of Osiris and think that even as the acacia grew about his body to protect it until Isis might find it; so does the acacia of Freemasonry bloom above the casket from which, in the solemn words of Ecclesiastes "the spirit shall return unto God who gave it."

Here are some comments from a Masonic book "A New Encyclopaedia of Freemasonry" by Arthur Edward Waite, P.M., P.Z., Past Senior Grand Warden of Iowa, Past Provincial Deputy Grand Director of Ceremonies (Bucks.), Past Grand Inner Guard (English Grand Mark), Past Great Captain of the Guards, Past Grand Historiographer, etc., etc., Author of "The Secret Tradition in Freemasonry, etc. pg. 1-3:-

Acacia

In so far as this Tree, which is connected with a memorable event in Masonic Legend, may be regarded as a symbol of immortality, the notion may be referred to its extraordinary persistence, for Du Pratz says that if any of the bark be left on its branches they will take root if planted as posts.

A Sign of Immortality.- It belongs to the analogies of hope beyond and life continued henceforward: it is to this that the Master-Mason testified, according to an old French Catechism, when in proof of his status he answered: "The Acacia is known to me." It has been said that it was consecrated to the sun in Arabia, but no evidence is offered.

In the Third Symbolical Grade, according to the classification adopted by the Masonic Order of Memphis, the Worshipful Master explains that "the Branch of Acacia…is an emblem of that ardent zeal for truth which should be cherished by every Master, encompassed as he is by corrupted men who betray it"; To sum up therefore, the emblem is – on the surface – funereal in Masonry, but in itself is a sign of life, and it has to be remembered that the great pageant with which it is connected is unquestionably one of resurrection. On such a priori considerations, the Acacia typifies that which is immortal in our nature; when planted to signify the place of rest where lay that which was perishable it testified that the Master lived, and so also that which denoted. The plans of the unfinished temple were not wanting but hidden; the Word was reserved somewhere and would be restored by time or circumstances; and after the shadowed lights of figurative resurrection, there would come the Orient light, the bright and morning-star, heralding a resurrection in the spirit, in the real and imperishable man, full of grace and truth. The motto to be inscribed on the Acacia is therefore Resurgamus nos.

A Sign of Innocence. – The Acacia in Greek is an axaxia, and the same word signifies simplicity, innocence and the mind turning from evil, as if with instinctive horror.

Edmond Ronayne comments in his book "The Master's Carpet" on the significance of the "Sprig of Accacia" in Masonry. Pg. 385-388;-

In witnessing Masonic funerals you have doubtless observed that every member of the fraternity carries a sprig of evergreen, which he finally deposits in the grave of the deceased with the exclamation, "Alas, my brother!" This evergreen is the acacia so often mentioned in the ritual of the Master Mason's degree, and which is supposed to have been planted at the head of the grave where Hiram's body is said to have been buried, and which also led to the accidental discovery of his remains. (See Handbook,

p. 210.) Concerning the origin of this Masonic emblem, and the reason why it occupies so prominent a position, both in the lodge and ritual we have the following explanation from our Masonic teachers. In the "Traditions of Freemasonry," by Pierson, p. 212.

"One fact is admitted, that the Masonic sprig (of acacia) is a substitute for the lotus, the Erica, the ivy, the myrtle, the mistletoe, etc., the sacred plant of the Ancient Mysteries."

This is precisely the very same evergreen shrub, or branch, which is also referred to in Ezekiel viii. 17, and the religious services and secret mysteries with which that emblem was associated in Jerusalem, by the idolatrous Jews, are precisely the same religious ceremonies, and the same secret mysteries, with which it is connected in our day in the Masonic lodge,

"Is it a light thing for the house of Judah," says Jehovah, speaking to the prophet, "that they commit the abominations which they commit here? For they have filled the land with violence, and have returned to provoke me to anger, and lo, they put the branch to their nose." (Ezekiel viii. 17.)

But, to conclude our investigation of the sublime (?) mysteries of Hiram Abiff, I shall offer a few more proofs, though in a collective form, from the emblems of the Master Mason's degree (and these shall be the last) to show that not even the most minute particular is wanting, to demonstrate the absolute identity of our modern system of Freemasonry with the old Baal, or Tammuz, or Osirian worship of the "mysteries."

The accompanying figure occupies a conspicuous and prominent place on the "MASTER'S CARPET" in every Masonic lodge room and in every Masonic Man-

ual of any note throughout the world. It consists, as we are informed in the ritual (see "Hand-book," p. 235), of a "beautiful virgin weeping over a broken column. Before her a book open; in her right hand an acacia, in her left an urn; behind her Time, standing, unfolding her ringlets and counting her hair." Now, what is the real origin of this figure? Who first introduced it into Masonry? And whence was the idea of this emblem borrowed?

Its true history is found in Pierson's "Traditions of Freemasonry," p. 220, as follows:

"Within the last fifty years there has been added to the American emblems of Freemasonry that which is sometimes termed a 'hieroglyphical figure'—a female weeping over a broken column, a book open before her; in her right hand a sprig, in her left an urn; Time standing behind her with his fingers enfolded in the ringlets of her hair. *This figure was designed* by the Rev. Jonathan Nye, for the *Hieroglyphic Monitor*, published by Jeremy L. Cross, in 1819. *The idea doubtless was aerived from the legend of Isis* weeping at Byblos, over the column torn from the palace of the king, which contained the body of Osiris, while *Horos*, the god of Time, pours ambrosia on her hair." (See p. 346.)

The Hieroglyphic Figure

The accompanying figure occupies a conspicuous and prominent place on the "Master's Carpet" in every Masonic lodge room and in every Masonic Manual of any note throughout the world.

It consists, as we are informed in the ritual (see "Hand-book," p. 235), of a "beautiful virgin weeping over a broken column. Before her a book open; in her right hand an acacia, in her left an urn; behind her Time, standing, unfolding her ringlets and counting her hair." Now, what is the real origin of this figure? Who first introduced it into Masonry? And whence was the idea of this emblem borrowed?

Its true history is found in Pierson's "Traditions of Freemasonry," p. 220, as follows:

"Within the last fifty years there has been added to the American emblems of Freemasonry that which is sometimes termed a 'hieroglyphical figure' – a female weeping over a broken column, a book open before her; in her right hand a sprig, in her left an urn; Time standing behind her with his fingers enfolded in the ringlets of her hair. This figure was designed by the Rev. Jonathan Nye, for the Hieroglyphic Monitor, published by Jeremy L. Cross, in 1819. The idea doubtless was arrived from the legend of Isis weeping at Byblos, over the column torn from the palace of the king, which contained the body of Osiris, while Horos, the god of Time, pours ambrosia on her hair." (See p. 346.)

"Lexicon of Freemasonry" – by Albert Gallatin Mackey, M.D. 330:-

Mackey says under the word "Acacian":-

"Acacian – a term signifying a Mason who by living in strict obedience to the obligations and precepts of the fraternity is free from sin."

Masonry teaches that obedience to Masonic obligations and precepts, which include no promotions or confession of any sectarian tenets such as Christianity, and embracing Freemasonry as the one true universal religion "in which all men agree", will make you "free from sin". Therefore, as a Mason in good standing upon death, the acacia twig or sprig of evergreen is placed in the casket at a Masonic funeral signifying his freedom from sin to live forever "in that Mother Lodge above.

But what does the Bible say of "justification by works" as opposed to" justification by faith in God's grace"?

Rom. iii. 24:-

"Being justified freely by his grace, through the redemption that is in Christ Jesus." Again in Gals. Ii. 16.

"Knowing that a man is not justified by the works of the law, but by the faith of Jesus Christ, even, we have believed in Jesus Christ that we might be justified by the faith of Christ and not by the works of the law, for by the works of the law shall no flesh be justified."

And again in Titus iii. 5.

"Not by works of righteousness which we have done but according to his mercy he saved us by the washing of regeneration and renewing of the Holy Ghost, which shed on us abundantly through Jesus Christ, our Saviour."

The following is from "The Masonic Report" by C.F. McQuaig, pg. 52, 53:-

40. Question: What in the mysteries of Masonry does the sprig of Acacia, or evergreen symbolize?

Answer: "In the ancient mysteries the coffin and the grave had a phallic signification, and is likewise true of them in Freemasonry. The dead Mason in the coffin, and the coffin with its contents, lowered into the grave, that is into the bosom of mother earth, is viewed as a conception which results in his birth into the Grand Lodge above. The sprig of acacia (evergreen), thrown into the grave, is remnant of tree and plant worship, symbolizes the female principle, which uniting with the Mason as the male principle, generates the immortal life."

41. Question: From what legend did Freemasonry draw its philosophy concerning the sprig of acacia?

Answer: From the legend of Osiris! "When Isis first found the body (of Osiris), where it had floated ashore near Byblos, a shrub of Erica or tamarisk near it had, by virtue of the body, shot up into a tree around it, and protected it; and hence our sprig of acacia." (Albert Pike's "Morals and Dogma," p. 376).

Ezekiel 8:18 says – "18. Therefore I will deal in wrath; my eye will not spare, nor will I have pity; and though they cry in MY ears with a loud voice, yet will I not hear them."

ADDENDUM

Parliament Hill: Ottawa

There needs to be exposure of the symbols and their hidden meanings throughout the Parliament Buildings for the following reasons:

1. That people who are influenced, oppressed by hidden darkness may come to GOD'S marvellous light! (Ephesians 5:11-14)
2. What Satan and willing men have erected in secret – has caused violence and sexual immorality to fill the land which must be reversed! (1 John 3:8)
3. I believe God is giving us due notice, in this season of the lowering of the Plumb line. Everything that can be aligned with God's word must be right-aligned, or we will experience God's judgement and wrath in this nation we hold dear!!! God's love, grace, and mercy always goes before judgement and wrath! But God demands justice and righteousness! (Psalm 89:11-16)
4. God has a PLAN and a PURPOSE for our Nation as a Leader in Peace, and Reconciliation, not Violence! (Jeremiah 18:5-10)

While I was doing my daily Bible reading in Second Chronicles, I felt the Lord speak to me concerning our Nation! In so many words, the Lord said to me, "Hezekiah was open to My Purpose and Plans for his day for Israel and Judah! I led Hezekiah each step of the way to lead the people is consecration to Me, to destroy the evil things they made and worshipped, that they might be victorious, and worship Me so I could bless them! (2 Chron. 31: 20, 21)

This is My desire, My DIVINE PLAN FOR CANADA also, as a Nation, TO RESTORE THE COVENANT I MADE WITH YOUR FOREFATHERS!"

Freemasonry: Ezekiel Chapter 8

The purpose of this Book is not a Commentary but an Expose to focus on the numerous similarities between the spirituality in Judah just before their captivity under Babylon and the spirit of Freemasonry!

> And in the sixth year (of the captivity of Jehoiachin), in the sixth month, on the fifth day of the month, as I sat in my house (a captive of the Babylonians) with the elders of Judah sitting before me, the hand of the Lord God fell there upon me. 2. Then I beheld, and lo, a likeness of a Man with the appearance of fire; from His waist downward He was like fire, and from his face upward He had the appearance of brightness like gleaming bronze. (Ezekiel 8:1-2)

This vision Ezekiel received from God was probably after he had lain 390 days on his left side to bear the iniquity of Israel and before he began the 40 days on his right side to bear the iniquity of Judah; for now he was sitting in the house, not lying down.

Also, can you imagine God giving Ezekiel a vision of why they are in captivity in Babylon and some of the elders of Judah sitting in the house with him might have been part of the group of elders in the vision?

1. Parliament Hill and the spirit of Baal/Freemasonry in light of Ezekiel's Vision of the "Image of Jealousy".
   Ezekiel 8:3 (b). says – "…..and the Spirit lifted me up between the earth and the heavens and brought me in the visions of God to Jerusalem, to the entrance of the door of the inner (court) which faces toward the north, where was the seat of the idol (image of jealousy, which provokes to jealousy."

On the south side of Parliament Hill, you enter the door which faces north and it takes you into the Entrance (the Rotunda). In the center of the Rotunda is a cylindrical column. As it rises upwards, multitudinal streams of smaller ones seem to spew out radially from the Central Column. Without going into much detail, as it has been discussed already, this is unmistakably a symbol of the Phallus (Male Generative Principle) whose essence brings forth life in the Female Passive Principle (eteis) in an everlasting sense through progressive procreation!

The image of the Sun around the Base or Seat of the idol (image) of jealousy is also present! The Phallus is the Male Principle in the Microcosm, while the "Sun" is the Male Principle in the Macrocosm!

Ezekiel 8:5(b) says – "…now lift up your eyes toward the north, and behold, on the north of the altar gate was that idol (image) of jealousy in the entrance."

The Holy Spirit shows Ezekiel "Looking North" from the Entrance (Rotunda), "on the North of the Altar Gate was that idol (Image) of Jealousy! Toward the North from the Rotunda outside the Parliament Block is the Library of Parliament. In the Lantern

Roof, you will see the Image of the "Sun" or the "Chariot of the Sun! The "Image of Jealousy" is "The Image of the Sun" at both locations – "where was the seat" and "lift up your eyes toward the north…entrance"!!!

The "Sun" is the "image of jealousy" which provokes to jealousy! The "Sun" is the chief deity in Baal Worship and in Freemasonry and had taken the place of God himself (the creator and Giver in all of Life) just before the captivity in Babylon! God was Israel's Husband and they provoked Him to jealousy – Hosea 2:16 says "16. And it shall be in that day, says the Lord, that you will call Me Ishi (my husband), and you shall call Me no more Baali (my Baal). Read the whole of Hosea Chapter 2!

Another very important area to be concerned about, besides the great abominations that have been committed, is what has been sown! Freemasonry/Baal Worship as has been demonstrated as the same spirit in Ezekiel 8 has filled our land with violence! Ezek. 8:17 (b) says – "…that they must fill the land with violence and turn back afresh to provoke Me to anger?"

Also, because of the multiplied numbers of Phallus symbols, circles, compasses, squares, triangles, star of Horus on the clock present and in "sexual Union" fashion, obviously promotes all kinds of sexual vice! As in the supernatural, so in the natural!

The "spiritual climate" in that day in Jerusalem will be "spiritually called Sodom and Egypt (amp.) I.e. the Egyptian Mysteries (the Risen Horus) and Phallus Worship! Rev. 11:8 (b) says – "….the great city which in a spiritual sense (by the mystical and allegorical names of) Sodom and Egypt…."

2. Parliament Hill and the spirit of Baal/Freemasonry in light of Ezekiel's Vision Chapter 8 and the Direction of North:-

First of all, the whole Vision from the Holy Spirit had to do with the men and women of Israel and Judah turning their backs to God and worshipping literally everything from the Sun to creeping things! But who is behind all this? Rev. 12:9 says – "And the huge dragon was cast down and out – that age-old serpent, who is called the Devil and Satan. He who is the seducer (deceiver) of all humanity the world over; he was forced out and down to the earth, and his angels were flung out along with him."

God said through Moses not to worship any other god(s)!!! Exodus 34:11-14 says – "11. Observe what I command you this day; I drive out before you the Amorite, Canaanite, Hittite, Perizzite, Hivite, and Jebusite. 12. Take heed to yourself, lest you make a covenant or agreement with the inhabitants of the land to which you go, lest it become a snare in the midst of you. 13. But you shall destroy their altars, dash in pieces their pillars, (obelisks, images), and cut down their Asherim (symbol of the goddess Asheran); 14. For you shall worship no other god; for the Lord, whose name is Jealous, is a jealous (impassioned) God, "but Lucifer's (Satan) goal was and still is to be worshipped like and as God! Matt. 4:9, 10 says – "And he said to him, these things, all taken together, I will give You, if You will prostrate Yourself before me and do homage and worship me. 10. Then Jesus said to him, Begone, Satan! For it has been written, you shall worship the Lord your God, and Him alone shall you serve."

Jesus is the Truth! John 14:6 says – "Jesus said to him, I am the Way and the Truth and the Life; no one comes to the Father except by (through) Me." But Satan seeks worship through lies, secrecy and deceit! 2 Cor. 4:3, 4 says "But even if our Gospel (the glad tidings be hidden (obscured and covered up with a veil that hinders the knowledge of God). it is hidden (only) to those who are perishing and obscured (only) to those who are lost. 4. For the god of this world has blinded the unbelievers' minds (that they should not discern the truth), preventing them from seeing the illuminating light of the Gospel of the glory of Christ (the Messiah), who is the Image and Likeness of God." The key document I quote here is an important, readily available, and universally accepted and approved doctrinal book of Freemasonry. It is called, "Morals and Dogma of the Ancient and Accepted Scottish Rite of Freemasonry" by Albert Pike, Sovereign Pontiff of Universal Freemasonry, and Grand Commander, 1859-1891. On pages 104, 105 he says – "Masonry, like all the religions, all the Mysteries, hermeticism and alchemy, conceals its secrets from all except the Adepts and Sages, or the Elect, and uses false explanations and mis-interpretations of its symbols to mislead those who deserve only to be misled, to conceal the Truth, which it calls light, from them, and to draw them away from it. This is not for those who are unworthy or unable to receive it, or would pervert it." Again, on page 819, Pike says – "The Blue Degrees are but the outer court or portico of the temple. Part of the symbols are displayed there to the Initiate but he is intentionally misled by false interpretations. It is not intended that he shall understand them, but it is intended that he shall imagine he understands them." The Ultimate god to be worshipped and adored in Freemasonry is Lucifer! I quote here from the booklet "The Question of Freemasonry" by J. Edward Decker Jr., author of "The God makers", pg. 11-14:-

Deities of Masonry

The Energies of Lucifer

"When the Mason learns that the Key to the warrior on the block is the proper application of the dynamo of living power, he has learned the Mystery of his Craft. The seething energies of Lucifer are in his hands and before he may step onward and upward, he must prove his ability to properly use (this) energy." (Lost Keys of Freemasonry, Manly P. Hall, page 48

DEITIES OF MASONRY

THE ENERGIES OF LUCIFER

"When the Mason learns that the Key to the warrior on the block is the proper application of the dynamo of living power, he has learned the Mystery of his Craft. The seething energies of LUCIFER are in his hands and before he may step onward and upward, he must prove his ability to properly apply [this] energy." (Lost Keys of Freemasonry, Manly P. Hall, page 48)

BAPHOMET. THE GOAT OF MENDES.

YES, LUCIFER IS GOD

"That which we must say to the crowd is—We worship a God, but it is the God that one adores without superstition.

"To you, Sovereign Grand Inspectors General, we say this, that you may repeat it to the Brethren of the 32nd, 31st, and 30th degrees—The Masonic Religion should be, by all of us initiates of the high degrees, maintained in the purity of the Luciferian Doctrine.

"If Lucifer were not God, would Adonay (The God of the Christians) whose deeds prove his cruelty, perfidy and hatred of man, barbarism and repulsion for science, would Adonay and his priests, calumniate him?

"Yes, Lucifer is God, and unfortunately Adonay is also god. For the eternal law is that there is no light without shade, no beauty without ugliness, no white without black, for the absolute can only exist as two gods: darkness being necessary for light to serve as its foil as the pedestal is necessary to the statue, and the brake to the locomotive.

"Thus, the doctrine of Satanism is a heresy; and the true and pure philosophical religion is the belief in Lucifer, the equal of Adonay; but Lucifer, God of Light and God of Good, is struggling for

humanity against Adonay, the God of Darkness and Evil." (Instructions to the 23 Supreme Councils of the World, Albert Pike, Grand Commander, Sovereign Pontiff of Universal Freemasonry, July 14, 1889. Recorded by A.C. De La Rive, La Femme et l'Enfant dans la Franc-Maconnerie Universelle, page 588)

Baphomet, the Goat of Mendes

Yes, Lucifer is God

"That which we must say to the crowd is – We worship a God, but it is the God that one adores without superstition.

"To you, Sovereign Grand Inspectors General, we say this that you may repeat it to the Brethren of the 32nd, 31st, and 30th degrees – The Masonic Religion should be, by all of us initiates of the high degrees, maintained in the purity of the Luciferian Doctrine.

"If Lucifer were not God, would Adonay (The God of the Christians) whose deeds prove his cruelty, perfidy and hatred of man, barbarism and repulsion for science, would Adonay and his priests, calumniate him?

"Yes, Lucifer is God, and unfortunately Adonay is also god. For the eternal law is that there is no light without shade, no beauty without ugliness, no white without black, for the absolute can only exist as two gods: darkness being necessary for light to serve as its foil as the pedestal is necessary to the statue, and the brake to the locomotive.

"Thus, the doctrine of Satanism is a heresy; and the true and pure philosophical religion is the belief in Lucifer, the equal of Adonay; but Lucifer, God of Light and God of Good is struggling for humanity against Adonay, the God of Darkness and Evil." (Instructions to the 23 Supreme Councils of the World, Albert Pike, Grand Commander, Sovereign Pontiff of Universal Freemasonry, July 14, 1889. Recorded by A.C. De La Rive, La Femme et L'Enfant dans la Franc-Maconnerie Universelle, page 599).

NOTE:- Occultists believe that "North" is the Place Where Governmental Authority Dwells"! Isaiah 9:6,7 says – "For to us a Child is born, to us a Son is given' and the government shall be upon His shoulder, and His name shall be called Wonderful Counsellor, Mighty God, Everlasting Father (of eternity), Prince of Peace. &. Of the increase of his government and of peace there shall be no end, upon the throne of David and over his kingdom, to establish it and to uphold it with justice and with righteousness from the (latter) time forth, even forevermore. The zeal of the Lord of Hosts will perform this." And Satan will be cast into the lake of fire! (Rev. 20:10). All Praise to God! Let everything that has breath, praise the Lord!!!

Below, is a daily Prayer Calendar from the Jerusalem House of Prayer based on the prophetic future of the 12 tribes mentioned in Ezekiel 48. Notice that the Tribe of Judah which camped on the East Side of the Tabernacle in the wilderness, will, in the future, be located at the North Gate of Jerusalem. Where Jesus will dwell among them as the Lion of the Tribe of Judah! Praise the Lord!!! Rev. 5:5 and Rev. 21:3.

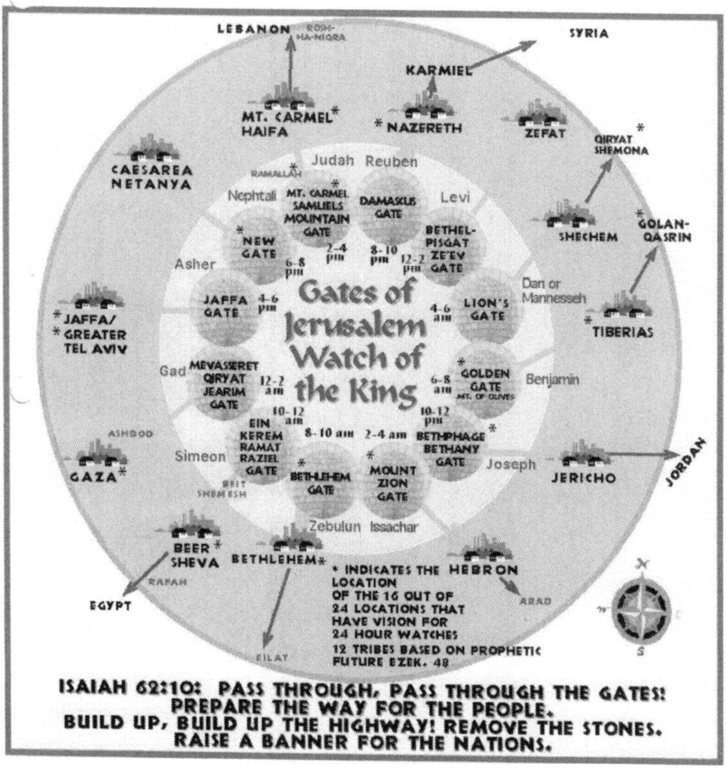

Gates of Jerusalem Watch of the King

Isaiah 62:10: Pass through, pass through the gates! Prepare the Way for the People.
Build up, Build Up the Highway! Remove the Stones. Raise a Banner for the Nations.

Prayer of Release for Freemasons and Their Descendants

Christians should pray for Masons without judging them. Bring their sins to God in an attitude of love, petitioning the Father for His mercy, binding the name of Jesus Christ the spirits of deception, antichrist, witchcraft and death. Please remember that "We do not wrestle against flesh and blood (your loved one) but against principalities, against powers against the rulers of the darkness of this world, against spiritual wickedness in high places," (Ephesians 6:12). This is a spiritual battle, and should be treated accordingly.

If you or someone you love is a descendant of a Mason, I recommend that you pray through the following prayer from your heart. Don't be like the Masons – please read it through first so you know what is involved. It is best to pray this aloud with a Christian witness or counsellor present.

"Father God, creator of heaven and earth, I come to you in the name of Jesus Christ your Son. I come as a sinner seeking forgiveness and cleansing from all sins committed against you, and others made in your image. I honour my earthly father and mother and all of my ancestors of flesh and blood, and of the spirit by adoption and godparents, but I utterly turn away from and renounce all their sins. I forgive all my ancestry for the effects of their sins on me and my children. I confess and renounce all of my own sins. I renounce and rebuke Satan and every spiritual power of his affecting me and my family.

I renounce and forsake all involvement in Freemasonry or any other lodge or craft by my ancestors and myself. I renounce witchcraft, the principal spirit behind Freemasonry, and I renounce Baphomet, the Spirit of Antichrist and the curse of the Luciferian doctrine. I renounce the idolatry, blasphemy, secrecy and deception of Masonry at every level. I specifically renounce the insecurity, the love of position and power, the love of money, avarice or greed, and the pride which would have led my ancestors into Masonry. I renounce all the fears which held them in Masonry, especially the fears of death, fears of men, and fears of trusting, in the name of Jesus Christ.

I renounce every position held in the lodge by one of my ancestors, including "Tyler," "Master," "Worshipful Master," or any other. I renounce the calling of any man "Master," for Jesus Christ is my only master and Lord, and He forbids anyone else having that title. I renounce the entrapping of others into Masonry, and observing the helplessness of others during the rituals. I renounce the effects of Masonry passed on to me through any female ancestor who felt destructed and rejected by her husband as he entered and attended any lodge and refused to tell her of his secret activities.

York Rite

I renounce the oaths taken and the cures involved in the York Rite of Freemasonry, including Mark Master, Past Master, Most Excellent Master, the Orders of the Red Cross, the Knights of Malta, and the Knights Templar degrees. I renounce the secret words of Joppa, Keb Raioth, and Maher-Shalal-Hash-Baz. I renounce the vows taken on a human skull the crossed swords, and the curse and death wish of Judas of having the head cut off and placed on top of a church spire. I renounce the unholy communion and especially drinking from a human skull in some Rites.

Shriner (America only – doesn't apply in other countries)

I renounce the oaths taken and the curses and penalties involved in the Ancient Arabic Order of the Nobles of the Mystic Shrine. I renounce the piercing of the eyeballs with a three-edged blade, the flaying of the feet, the madness, and the worship of the false god Allah as the god of our fathers. I renounce the hoodwink, the mock hanging, the mock beheading, the mock drinking of the blood of the victim, the mock dog urinating on the initiate, and the offering of urine as a commemoration.

33rd Degree

I renounce the oaths taken and the curses involved in the thirty-third degree of Masonry, the Grand Sovereign Inspector General. I renounce and forsake the declaration that Lucifer is God. I renounce the calbe-tow around the neck. I renounce the death wish that the wine drunk from a human skull should turn to poison and the skeleton whose cold arms are invited if the oath of this degree is violated. I renounce the three infamous assassins of their grand master, law, property and religion, and the greed and witchcraft involved in the attempt to manipulate and control the rest of mankind.

All Other Degrees

I renounce all the other oaths taken, the rituals of every other degree and the curses involved. I renounce all other lodges and secret societies such as Prince Hall Freemasonry Mormonis, The Order of Amaranth, Oddfellows, Buffalos, Druids, Foresters, Orange, Elks, Moose and Eagles Lodges, the Ku Klux Klan. The Grange, the Woodmen of the World, Roders of the Red Robe, the Knights of Pythias, the Mystic Order of the Veiled Prophets of the Enchanted Realm, the women's Orders of the Eastern Star and of the White Shrine of Jerusalem, the girls' order of the Daughters of the Eastern Star, the International Orders of Job's Daughters, and of the Rainbow, and the boys' Order of De Molay and their effects on me and all my family.

I renounce the ancient pagan teaching and symbolism of the First Tracing Board, the Second Tracing Board and the Third Tracing Board used in the ritual of the Blue Lodge. I renounce the pagan ritual of the "Point within a Circle" with all its bondages and phallus worship. I renounce the occultic mysticism of the black and white mosaic chequered floor with the tessellated boarder and five-pointed blazing star. I renounce the symbol "G" and its veiled pagan symbolism and bondages. I renounce and utterly forsake the Great Architect of the Universe, who is revealed in the higher degrees as Lucifer, and his false claim to be the universal fatherhood of God. I also renounce the false claim that Lucifer is the Morning Star and Shining One and I declare that Jesus Christ is the Bright and Morning Star of Revelation 22:16.

I renounce the All-Seeing Third Eye of Freemasonry or Horus in the forehead and its pagan and occult symbolism. I renounce all false communions taken, all mockery of the redemptive work of Jesus Christ on the cross of Calvary, all unbelief, confusion and depression, and all worship of Lucifer as God. I renounce and forsake the life of Freemasonry that man is not sinful, but just imperfect, and so can redeem himself through good works. I rejoice that the Bible states that I cannot do a single thing to earn my salvation, but that I can only be saved by grace through faith in Jesus Christ and what He accomplished on the cross of Calvary.

I renounce all fear of insanity, anguish, death wishes, suicide and death in the name of Jesus Christ. Death was conquered by Jesus Christ, and He alone holds the keys of death and hell, and I rejoice that He holds my life in His hands now. He came to give me life abundantly and eternally, and I believe His promises.

I renounce all anger, hatred, murderous thoughts, revenge, retaliation, spiritual apathy, false religion, all unbelief, especially unbelief in the Holy Bible as God's Word, and all compromise of God's Word. I renounce all spiritual searching into false religions, and all striving to please God. I rest in the knowledge that I have found my Lord and Saviour Jesus Christ, and that He has found me.

I will burn all objects in my possession which connect me with all lodges and occultic organizations including Masonry, Witchcraft and Mormonism, and all regalia, aprons, books of rituals, rings and other jewellery. I renounce the effects these or other objects of Masonry, such as the compass, the square, the noose or the blindfold have had on me or my family, in Jesus Name.

Holy Spirit, I ask that you show me anything else which I need to do or to pray so that I and my family may be totally free from the consequences of the sins of Masonry, Witchcraft, Mormonism and Paganism.

(Pause, while listening to God, and pray as the Holy Spirit leads you.)

Now dear Father God, I ask humbly for the blood of Jesus Christ, your Son, to cleanse me from all these sins I have confessed and renounced, to cleanse my spirit, my soul, my mind, my emotions and every part of my body which has been affected by these sins, in Jesus' name!

I renounce every evil spirit associated with Masonry and Witchcraft and all other sins, and I command in the name of Jesus Christ for Satan and every evil spirit to be bound and to leave me now, touching or harming no-one, and go to the place appointed for you by the Lord Jesus, never to return to me or my family. I call on the name of the Lord Jesus to be delivered of these spirits, in accordance with the many promises of the Bible. I ask to be delivered of every spirit of sickness, infirmity, curse, affliction, addiction, disease or allergy associated with these sins I have confessed and renounced.

I surrender to God's Holy Spirit and to no other spirit all the places in my life where these sins have been. I ask you, Lord, to baptise me in your Holy Spirit now according to the promises in your Word. I take to myself the whole armour of God in accordance with Ephesians Chapter Six, and rejoice in its protection as Jesus surrounds me and fills me with His Holy Spirit. I enthrone you, Lord Jesus, in my heart, for you are my Lord and my Saviour, the source of eternal life. Thank you, Father of God, for your mercy, your forgiveness and your love, in the name of Jesus Christ, Amen."

Jubilee Ministries Trust (Incorporated)
(A registered charity in New Zealand)
P.O. Box 36-044, Wellington 6330
Phone/Fax 64-4-568-4533

Reference/Bibliography

"Comparative Study Bible", Zondervan Publishing House, Grand Rapids, Michigan, 1999

"Morals and Dogma of the Ancient and Accepted Scottish Rite of Freemasonry", Published in 1871. (Masonic)

"Encyclopedia of Freemasonry", by Albert Mackey, Volume 1 Published in 1914, Volume 2 Published in 1916. (Masonic)

"A New Encyclopedia of Freemasonry", by Arthur Edward Waite, P.M., P.Z., 1891. (Masonic)

"The Masters Carpet", (MAH – HAH – BONE) or Masonry and Baal Worship Identical, by Edmond Ronayne, 1879. (Non – Masonic)

"Beyond the Pillars (More Light on Freemasonry)", Edited by the Special Committee on Publications, Grand Lodge A.F. and A.M. of Canada in the Province of Ontario, Published by the Authority of the Grand Master, Jan.1, 1973. (Masonic)

"Whence Come We?, Freemasonry in Ontario 1764 – 1980", Edited by the Special Committee on the History, Wallace McLeod, Chairman, Published by Authority of the Grand Master. (Masonic)

"The Two Babylons or the Papal Worship", by the late Alexander Hislop, first edition 1916, Published in America by Loizeau Brothers, Inc.. (Non – Masonic)

"The Masonic Report", by Cecil F. McQuaig, Published by Answer Books and Tapes, 5166 Old Norcross Road, Norcross, Georgia, 30071. (Non – Masonic)

"Lost Keys of Freemasonry", by Manly P. Hall, Macoy Publishing and Masonic Supply Co., Richmond, Virginia, 1976. (Masonic)

"Jubillee Ministries Trust (Incorporated)", (A registered Charity in New Zealand), P.O. Box 36-044, Wellington 6330. (Non – Masonic)

"Constitution of the Ancient Fraternity of Free and Accepted Masons", by William Williams, Esq., 1823. (Masonic)

"Lexicon of Freemasonry", by Albert Mackey, 1869. (Masonic)

"Divine Ligation", by William Warburton, Published Dec.9, 2013. (Masonic)

"Ahiman Rezon", by Daniel Sickles, 1744. (Masonic)

"Digest of Masonic Law", by George Wingate Chase, Published on Aug. 12, 2015. (Masonic)

"Manual of the Lodge", by Albert Mackey Published in 1862. (Masonic)

"Traditions of Freemasonry", by Pierson, Published in 1863. (Masonic)

"Symbolism of Freemasonry", by Albert Mackey, Published in 1882. (Masonic)

"The Masonic Report", by C.F. McQuaig with Introduction and Lecture of the 32nd degree by James D. Shaw 33rd. Degree Mason. No publication date. (Non – Masonic)

"Egyptian Mysteries", by Sharp, no Publication date. (Masonic)

"Moses and Aaron", by Thomas Godwyn Published in 1698. (Masonic)

"The Ancient and Accepted Scottish Rite", by Wingate, Published 1914. (Masonic)

"Occult Theocracy", by Lady Queensborough (Edith Starr Miller), Published Posthumously by the Christian Book Club of America, 1933. (Non – Masonic)

Other Recommended Books

"The Return of the GODS", by Jonathan Cahn (From the New York Times Best Selling Author), Published by Front Line, 600 Rinechart Road, Lake Mary, Florida 32746.

"The Protocols of Zion" (Otherwise called "The Protocols of the meetings of the LEARNED ELDERS OF ZION), by Victor E. Marsden, Published 1934. Note: Masonry is mentioned multiple times in almost every Protocol which indicates the heavy use of Masons to realize their goals for world dominance!!!

"Proofs of a Conspiracy" by John Robison, A.M., Published in 1798, Published by Western Islands, Belmont, Massachusetts.

"The Unseen Hand" (An Introduction to the Conspiratorial View of History" by A. Ralph Epperson, Published in 1985 by Publius Press, 3100 South Philamena Place, Suite B, Tucson, Arizona, 85730.

"The New World Order", by A. Ralph Epperson, Published in 1990 by Publius Press.

"The Dark Side of Freemasonry", by Ed Decker with Angelina Stanford McBride, Published in 1994 by Huntinghouse Publishers.

"Freemasonry: The Invisible Cult in Our Midst" by Jack Harris (A former Worshipful Master), Published in 1983 by Jack Harris, P.O. Box 20214, Towson, MD 21204.

"The United Nations Conspiracy" by Robert W. Lee, Published in 1981 by Western Islands, 395 Concord Ave., Belmont, Massachusetts 02178

"The Shadows of Power (The Council on Foreign Relations and the American Decline), by James Perloff, Published in 1988 by Western Islands, Appleton, Wisconsin.

"Towards World Government (New World Order)", by Deirdre Manifold, Published in 1990 by Firinne Publications, 15 Dalysfort, Galway.

"Secret Societies and Subversive Movements" by Nesta H. Webster, Published in 1924 by Christian Book Club of America.

"The Deadly Deception" (Freemasonry Exposed…By one of its top Leaders)", by Jim Shaw (33rd Degree, Knight Commander of the Court of Honor, Past Worshipful Master in the Blue Lodge, Past Master of all Scottish Rite bodies), Published 1988 by Tom McKenny and Huntington House, P.O. Box 53788, Lafayette, Louisiana 70505.

"I Left the Lodge" (a former Mason)", by Dale A. Byers, Published 1937 by Regular Baptist Press, 1300 North Meacham Road, Schaumburg, Illinois 60173 – 4888.

"The Brotherhood" (The explosive expose of the secret world of the Freemasons), by Stephen Knight, Published in 1983 by Grafton Books, a Division of the Collins Publishing Group, London, Glascow, Toronto, Sydney, Auckland.

"Behind the Lodge Door", by Paul A. Fisher, Published in 1988 by Shield Publishing, Inc., Bowie, MD.

"Destruction of Freemasonry (Through Revelation of their Secrets)", by General Erich Ludendorff, Published in 1927 by The Noontide Press, P.O. Box 76062, Los Angeles, CA 90005.

"Darkness Visible" (A Christian Appraisal of Freemasonry), by Walton Hannah, Published in 1952 by Augustine Publishing Company, Chulmleigh Devon, EX 18 7HL, UK.

"Christ, The Christian and Freemasonry", Published in 1984 by Great Joy Publications, 12 Ballynahinch Road, Carryduff, Belfast, BT8 8DN or from Saints Alive In Jesus, P.O. Box 1076, Issaquah, W.A. 98027, U.S.A.

"Lodges Examined by the Bible" by John R. Rice, Published in 1943 by Sword of the Lord Publishers, U.S.A.

"The Character, Claims and Practical Workings of Freemasonry, by Charles G. Finney, Entered by Act of Congress in 1869 and republished 1998 by Jon Kregel, Inc., dba, JKI Publishing, Tyler, Texas 75713.

"Should a Christian be a Mason?" by E. M. Storms, Published in 1980 by New Puritan Library.

"The Southern Baptist Convention and Freemasonry" Published in 1992 by Mission and Ministry to Men, Inc.,550 North Tenth Street, Beaumont, Texas, 77706.

"Freemasonry and the Vatican" (A Struggle for Recognition)" by Vicomte Leon De Poncin and Published in 1917 by CONGRES des Maconneries des NationsAlliees et neuters.

"Millenium" (Peace, Promises, and the Day They Take Our Money Away) by Texe Marrs, Published in 1990 by Living Truth Publishers, 8103 Shiloh Court, Austin, Texas 78745.

"Grand Orient Freemasonry Unmasked (as the SECRET POWER behind COMMUNISM) BY Mgr: George E. Dillon, D.D., Published in October 1884, delivered by Rev. Denis Fahey, C.S. Sp., B. A., D. Ph., D.D. (Professor of Philosophy and Church History), Published by Sons of Liberty, Box 214, Meteirie, LA 70004.

"The Signs and Symbols of Primordial Man" (The Evolution of Religious Doctrines From The Eschatology of The Ancient Egyptians), by Albert Churchward, M.D., M.R.C.P., M.R.C.S., F.G.S., P.M., P.Z. 30 degree Mason and also Author of "Origin and Antiquity of Freemasonry", etc., Published in 1913 by Greenwood Press, Publishers, Westport, Connecticut (Reprinted from an original copy in the collection of the Lucis Trust Library). NOTE: A deeply Masonic book that should leave you with no doubt that Masonry and Christianity is not compatible!!!